# 1001
## Surprising Things
## You Should Know
## about the Bible

# 1001
## Surprising Things You Should Know about the Bible

Jerry MacGregor and Marie Prys

**Baker Books**
A Division of Baker Book House Co
Grand Rapids, Michigan 49516

© 2002 by Jerry MacGregor and Marie Prys

Published by Baker Books
a division of Baker Book House Company
P.O. Box 6287, Grand Rapids, MI 49516-6287

Second printing, April 2003

Printed in the United States of America

Library of Congress Cataloging-in-Publication Data
MacGregor, Jerry.
    1001 surprising things you should know about the Bible / Jerry MacGregor and Marie Prys.
        p.    cm.
    Includes bibliographical references and index.
    ISBN 0-8010-6424-4 (pbk.)
    1. Bible—Miscellanea.  I. Title: one thousand and one surprising things you should know about the Bible.  II. Title: One thousand one surprising things you should know about the Bible.  III. Prys, Marie.  IV. Title.
    BS615 .M23   2002
    220—dc21                                                    2002009124

For current information about all releases from Baker Book House, visit our web site:

http://www.bakerbooks.com

For Kambiz Mirsepassi,
with thanks for your friendship
—Chip

For my family—
immediate, extended, and inherited—
one of life's greatest gifts
—Marie

# Contents

# Introduction

It's the best-selling book of all time—a volume that has changed the course of history, affected the lives of millions, and made all of us stop and think. Christian martyrs have died for reading this precious volume. It's been hidden, suppressed, and exalted through the ages. Though the authors lived thousands of years apart and included kings, shepherds, prophets, humble fishermen, and well-educated apostles, this book speaks to *every* person.

The Bible also holds the key to the most famous person the world has ever seen or known—Jesus Christ. It tells us where we came from and directs us where we may ultimately go. Why do we read this book? *To know God.* To meet him, commune with him, and find peace with him. Along the way, we discover amazing prophecies, inspiring stories, and truly horrible happenings that changed history forever.

*1001 Surprising Things You Should Know about the Bible* illuminates the many characters, events, and exciting facts about the most influential book ever written in the history of the world. This collection is not made up of the 1001 "most important" facts, the 1001 "best" facts, or even what we might consider the 1001 "most necessary for a complete education" facts. Rather we have picked what is unique, unfamiliar, and might not be included in a scholarly examination of the Bible . . . yet what is indeed still a part of it. All 1001 facts were checked and considered, but this isn't what you might consider a "researched" volume. Instead it's fun. And true.

No book *about* the Bible will ever be a substitute for the original, inspired Word of God. So we pray *this* book will be used and enjoyed for its information, but that the Bible's authority will always remain primary in your life.

Jerry MacGregor and Marie Prys

Part I

# How *the Bible* Came to Be

# 1

# About the Bible

**1. The Bible.** Christians believe this book to be the true Word of God. From the creation account of Genesis to the end-time visions of Revelation, from the story of Israel to Jesus' ministry, it is the source for what Christians believe and how they try to live.

**2. The word *Bible*** comes from the Greek word *biblia,* which means "books," which comes from another word, *byblos,* meaning papyrus, a material books were made from in ancient times.

**3. The ancient Greeks obtained their supplies of paper from the port of Byblos,** in what is now Lebanon. Their word for book—*biblion* (the singular form of *biblia*)—was derived from the name of this port, and from this we get our English word *Bible,* meaning the Book of books.

**4. The word *Bible*** is not in the Bible. The term came long after all the writings were completed and assembled.

**5. The Bible** is the world's best-selling book as well as the world's most shoplifted book!

**6. The Bible is the most bought** yet least understood book. Nine out of ten Americans own a Bible, but fewer than half ever read it. Worldwide sales of the Bible are uncountable.

**7. Just how big is the Bible?** Stack ten average-sized nonfiction books printed today. That pile will contain the same number of words that are found in one Bible—close to one million words not counting the number of words in features like footnotes, verse numbers, and concordances.

**8. The Bible looks like one book,** but it is actually an anthology, a collection of many smaller books. In an even broader sense, it is not just an anthology of shorter works but an entire library.

**9. Some Bible books are as short as half a page.** One of the longest books—Jeremiah—is roughly the length of today's short novel. This makes the Bible's longest book one hundred times longer than its shortest book.

**10. Though the Bible as a whole** is much longer than most any other book we'd like to read, its individual books are mostly shorter than any other book we consider reading.

**11. The Bible is an extraordinary gathering** of many books of law, wisdom, poetry, philosophy, and history. The number of books in this portable library depends on which Bible you are holding. The Bible of a Jew is different from the Bible of a Roman Catholic, which in turn is different from the Bible of a Protestant.

**12. The Bible is both ancient and contemporary** as it deals with the unchanging issues of human existence: life, death, joy, sorrow, achievement, and failure. . . . Yet these issues are couched in the language and correspondence of ancient times.

**13. *Testament*** was another word for "covenant"—meaning an agreement, contract, or pact. For Christians, the Old Testament represents the ancient covenant made between God and his people.

In the New Testament, Christians believe in a new covenant with God made through the life, death, and resurrection of Jesus.

**14. Written over the course of a thousand years,** primarily in ancient Hebrew, the Jewish Bible is the equivalent of Christianity's Old Testament. For Jews there is no New Testament.

**15. At least half as much time elapsed** between the Bible's first book and its last (with well over a thousand years between the first writing and the time of the last), as has elapsed between its last book and now. This means that writing styles vary not just between modern books and the Bible but among the Bible books themselves.

**16. The terms *Old Testament* and *New Testament* originated with** the prophet Jeremiah. When he spoke about the glorious future for Israel of which the prophets often spoke, he said that God would "make a new covenant with the house of Israel." Testament means "covenant," and Jesus of Nazareth, the long-awaited Messiah, made a new covenant with God's people. The books of the New Testament provide the fulfillment of the promises made throughout the Old Testament books.

**17. The translation of the Hebrew Scriptures** into the *Koine* Greek dialect was an outstanding literary accomplishment under the Ptolemies. This translation was called the *Septuagint*. The translation project is said to have been sponsored by Ptolemy II Philadelphus around the third century B.C. According to tradition, seventy-two Jewish scholars (six from each of the twelve tribes) were summoned for the project. The work was finished in seventy-two days; the Jewish scholars were then sent away with many gifts.

**18. The Septuagint** provided a bridge between the thoughts and vocabulary of the Old and New Testaments. The language of the New Testament is not the *koine* of the everyday Greek, but the *koine* of the Jew living in Greek surroundings. By the New Testament era, it was the most widely used edition of the Old Testament.

**19. Most Jews of Jesus' day spoke Aramaic,** a Syrian language similar to Hebrew that was commonly used at the time. Jesus surely studied the formal Hebrew of the Torah, Prophets, and Writings.

Whether he could also speak Greek is unknown. Jesus left no personal writings.

**20. Both the Jewish Bible and Christian Old Testament** contain the same thirty-nine books, although they are arranged and numbered in a slightly different order. In Jewish traditions the Bible is called the *Tanakh,* an acronym of the Hebrew words *Torah* (for "law" or "teaching"), *Nevi'im* ("the Prophets"), and *Kethuvim* ("the Writings").

**21. The Old Testament's** first five books, the Pentateuch, were already considered authoritative Scripture by the time of Ezra in the fifth century B.C. The other books were recognized as part of the Old Testament at later times.

**22. Jesus himself knew the "old covenant."** As a Jewish boy, he diligently studied the Torah, Prophets, and Writings. He could recite them by heart when he was twelve. Because there was no Bible as we know it, he would have learned by rote from scrolls kept by local teachers or rabbis.

**23. The earliest references to the Old Testament** were "the law of Moses," "the law of the Lord," or simply "Moses." Since the additional writings were considered the work of prophets, the common term became "Moses and the Prophets" or something similar. *Note: Wherever the word "law" is seen, the Jewish reference would be "Torah."* By New Testament times, "Scripture" or "the Scriptures" became common. The simplest generic term for the collection was "writings," often with "sacred" or "holy" added.

**24. The uniformity of Bible printing** sometimes obscures the scope of variety within the Bible's writings. If Bible printers laid out the print with all the different styles and languages accounted for, including prose, poetry, and songs, a wheelbarrow would be needed to move a Bible from the den to the bedroom.

**25. No Bible writer that we know of ever drew a map** to accompany his writing—at least not one that was preserved. Maps are generally drawn from facts discovered through historical and archaeological research.

# 2

# Nuts and Bolts

**26. Jerome** (340–420) began his ascetic lifestyle as a hermit but found he needed something to occupy his mind. He took up Hebrew and eventually began teaching classes in biblical interpretation. In A.D. 382 he would translate the Old and New Testaments from their original languages (Hebrew and Greek) into Latin—what we call the "Vulgate."

**27. The tests of canonicity** included: (1) the book had to have a history of being used in Christian worship; (2) the book had to be written by an apostle, or associated with an apostle; and (3) the book had to have evidenced power in the lives of believers.

**28. No New Testament.** During the entire first century and much of the second century there was no concept of a New Testament canon. Church fathers often quoted from sources that were familiar in tone yet different in the names of the sources. Paul's writings were the most well known and were quoted often, but they were not thought of as scriptural.

**29. The term** *New Testament* was created by Tertullian around the year 200. In an attempt to move the church away from Greek and toward Latin, which had become the preferred language of scholars, Tertullian referred to the writings of the Christian church as *Novum Testamentum*—a phrase we still employ today. Interestingly Tertullian also coined the term *Trinity* to refer to the Father, Son, and Holy Spirit.

**30. A New Testament Canon** was not looked upon favorably at first. In fact it was through heretical movements that the New Testament came into being as a legitimate part of the Holy Bible. Marcion was a teacher who broke away from the church in Rome. Around A.D. 150 he rejected the Old Testament and instead chose to accept only ten letters from Paul along with the Gospel of Luke as authoritative Christian Scripture.

**31. The Muratorian Canon** is named for its discoverer, L. A. Muratori, who first published it in 1740. A fascinating look into the early church, it reveals that by the year 190, Christians had developed their own New Testament and put it alongside the Jewish Scriptures—the former the fulfillment of the latter. It contains in order: Matthew, Mark, Luke, John, Acts, 1 and 2 Corinthians, Ephesians, Philippians, Colossians, Galatians, 1 and 2 Thessalonians, Romans, Philemon, Titus, 1 and 2 Timothy, the Apocalypse of John (Revelation), the Apocalypse of Peter, and the Wisdom of Solomon.

**32. Some books of Scripture faced challenges.** Christians in the West didn't like Hebrews, while those in the East opposed Revelation. Church historian Eusebius, writing in the fourth century, noted that James, 2 Peter, 2 and 3 John, Jude, and Revelation were the only books "spoken against." Martin Luther would challenge the Book of James in the sixteenth century, calling it "an epistle of straw."

**33. Accepted at last.** The Eastern church accepted the New Testament as we know it in A.D. 367 with the 39th Paschal Letter of Athanasius, and the Western church followed suit after Pope Damascus called a synod together in Rome in 382.

**34. The allegorical method** of interpretation went to extreme lengths to try to make the Old Testament into a Christian book. Origen, one of the first Christian theologians, believed that "the Scriptures were composed through the Spirit of God, and have both a meaning which is obvious and another which is hidden." He then proceeded to create all sorts of allegorical meanings to the Word of God—infuriating his critics, who felt that Origen was crafting theological implications out of thin air.

**35. We get our word** *paper* from the papyrus plant—a tall weed that could be cut into strips, flattened, then woven together and dried to form sheets of paper. It is incredibly resilient, and scraps of paper with Scripture on them date back to the early second century. Writing done on sheepskin was known as "parchment."

**36. In ancient times when parchment was too expensive** to possess, peasants would use fragments of pottery to write (scratch) memoranda of business transactions. Many of these have been uncovered by archaeologists, and they reveal much about ancient history. These fragments are called ostraca.

**37. The word translated "book"** in your Bible is really the word for "scroll." The words of Scripture were written onto pieces of parchment or papyrus; then those pieces were glued together to form scrolls. It wasn't until the second century that the notion of "pages" was invented, when a "codex" was created by gluing several flat sheets to a wooden spine.

**38. The Bible wasn't translated into English** until the seventh century A.D. The translations weren't precise at that point—they read more as a paraphrasing of the original manuscripts. The copies were known as "manuscript Bibles," and few have survived.

**39. Florilegia** were popular with the masses before the invention of movable type. Artists would create a collection of Bible verses and pictures, often on one particular topic, and produce them in quantities. These small booklets (which get their name from the Latin phrase "to gather flowers") were then used to teach basic Christian doctrine to groups of people.

**40. The Glosses** were Latin Bibles in which a scholar had taken a pen and written a translation into another language. This was generally done in secret because the Roman Catholic Church had banned Bibles in any language but Latin. By writing a literal translation of each word, those who did it were "glossing" or "explaining" foreign words to future readers. Their notes, written above each line of Latin type, gave rise to the expression "reading between the lines."

**41. The Lindisfarne Gospels** are one such manuscript Bible that has survived. It was written in Latin around A.D. 700, but it has an English interlinear translation that was added into the original 250 years later.

**42. The earliest known *fragment* of a New Testament papyrus manuscript** was recovered from the ruins of a Greek town in ancient Egypt. A mere 2-1/2 inches by 3-1/4 inches, the fragment dates from about A.D. 115 or 125 and contains a portion of John 18:31–33, 37–38. It is commonly called the Rylands Fragment because it is housed in the John Rylands Library of Manchester, England.

**43. The Codex Sinaiticus** is the oldest copy of the complete New Testament. Housed in the British Museum in London, it contains handwritten pages bound to a spine on one side. Written in Greek, it dates from about the year A.D. 350.

**44. Count Constantine von Tischendorf** discovered the Codex Sinaiticus at the Monastery of Saint Catherine on Mount Sinai in 1859. It was written in large Greek letters (uncials) on vellum sheets that measured fifteen by thirteen inches wide. It had been copied in the fourth century A.D., making it the earliest complete copy of the New Testament in existence. Many other manuscripts were written earlier, but they were not complete copies.

**45. The Book of Kells** is an illuminated manuscript—that is, a lavishly decorated, handwritten copy—of the four Gospels in Latin. Produced in Ireland, it is generally regarded as the most beautiful handcrafted book of all time.

# 3

# How the Bible Reads

**46. More than three thousand** versions of the entire Bible, or portions of it, exist in English.

**47. Chapter and verse divisions in the Bible were not determined** by those who wrote the words we read. These divisions were added to the text hundreds of years after the authors died. The original writers neither planned nor anticipated these divisions.

**48. Chapter and verse numbers** in the apostles' letters, for example, would appear as strange to them as the following does to us:

Dear Aunt Sue,

Chapter One

Last week we went to town and learned that . . .

**49. "Divided on horseback"** was the criticism of Robert Estienne, a French publisher and convert to Protestantism who decided to number the verses in the New Testament in order to make it easier to study and memorize. While Stephen Langton had divided the text into chapters, Estienne then broke each chapter into numbered verses. According to his son, he did much of the work while on horseback—leading critics ever since to suggest the reason some verses' divisions are short and others are long was because of the bumpy ride between his office in Paris and his home in southern France.

**50. The Bible was designed more for the ear than the eye.** In antiquity people passed history and genealogy from generation to generation by oral tradition—through storytelling or by reading aloud. Those who wrote the Bible did so knowing that their words would be read aloud. So puns, acrostics, and cryptograms are all used widely throughout the Hebrew Scriptures.

**51. Mgn rdng ths bk wtht vwls.** Myb ftr whl y cld fll n sm f th blnks nd fgr t mst f t. Ftr ll, t's smpl nglsh. Bt nw, mgn t s prt f n ncnt lngg tht hs flln nt dss vr svrl cntrs. Tht s hw th Bbl nc pprd. Imagine reading this book without vowels. Maybe after a while you could fill in some of the blanks and figure out most of it. After all, it's simple English. But now, imagine it as part of an ancient language that has fallen into disuse over several centuries. That is how the Bible once appeared.

**52. Hieroglyphics**—derived from two Greek words that mean "sacred carvings," since the signs were at first chiseled on stone—were the basic writing system in Egypt at the time of Moses. Since young Moses was educated in the Egyptian sciences and arts, he no doubt learned to read and write Egyptian hieroglyphics. About 750 pictures were used at first in hieroglyphics. At least twenty-two signs existed for various birds, such as the curved neck of the Egyptian vulture, the flat face of an owl, and the tail feathers of the pintail duck.

**53. The alphabet's origin.** A few hundred years after the time of Moses, the Phoenicians invented an alphabet. They took the Egyptian syllabic signs and used each to represent a single sound. The Phoenicians and the Hebrews used only twenty-two symbols and had no letters for vowels.

**54. The alphabet quickly** spread throughout the Mediterranean world colonized by the Phoenicians. About 800 B.C. it was transmitted to the Greeks, who improved it by adding vowels. This is the alphabet that spread to the Romans, who passed it on to us almost in its present form.

**55. The Hebrew alphabet** has twenty-two letters, all of them consonants. In fact Semitic languages like Hebrew, Aramaic, and Arabic are still generally written without any vowels, although a system of dots and dashes above and below the line of writing has been added in recent times to aid in knowing what vowels are needed. Readers of classical Hebrew were and are versed in its oral traditions and provide the vowel sounds from memory.

**56. When the Old Testament writers completed their scrolls,** they depended on scribes, men who patiently copied the Scriptures by hand when extra copies were needed and when the original scrolls became too worn to use any longer. By the time Jesus was born, the books of Moses had been copied and recopied over a span of more than fourteen hundred years!

**57. Before beginning his work each day,** a scribe would test his reed pen by dipping it in ink and writing the word *Amalek* and then crossing it out (cf. Deut. 25:19). Then he would say, "I am writing the Torah in the name of its sanctity and the name of God in its sanctity."

**58. The scribe would read a sentence** in the manuscript he was copying, repeat it aloud, and then write it. Each time he came to the name of God, he would say, "I am writing in the name of God for the holiness of his name." If he made an error in writing God's name, the scribe had to destroy the entire sheet of papyrus or vellum that he was using.

**59. After the scribe finished copying a particular book,** he would count all the words and letters it contained. Then he checked this tally against the count for the manuscript that he was copying. He counted the number of times a particular word occurred in the book, and he noted the middle word and the middle letter in the book, comparing all of these with the original. By making these careful checks, he hoped to avoid any scribal errors.

**60. The Bible was written in several languages.** Most of the Old Testament books are in Hebrew, but parts of Daniel are in Aramaic. The New Testament books are written in *koine* ("common") Greek, though they contain Latin, Aramaic, and Hebrew phrases.

**61. The Masoretes** were a group of Jewish scholars who wanted to ensure that the Old Testament documents would not become corrupted over time. Since the Hebrew language has no vowels, they created a system of inserting "vowel points" into the text to help priests and readers know how to pronounce the words properly. Their careful work has led to almost no changes in Old Testament wording for more than a millennium. Translators today still refer to the "Masoretic" text.

**62. The Hebrew language** slowly changed, as languages do, throughout the centuries after the Old Testament writers passed away. The language of Moses would seem strange to a modern Israeli, just as the language of Chaucer or even Shakespeare is difficult for us to discern.

**63. The Greeks,** who borrowed the basic twenty-two-letter alphabet used in Hebrew and Phoenician, added five new letters at the end of their alphabet. These five additional letters are the reason why the Greeks are credited for inventing the vowel system.

**64. Approximately two thousand years of history** pass within the Bible's pages. Great empires came and went around the ancient Near East: Sumer, Akkadia, Babylon, Egypt, Assyria, Persia, and Greece. Along with those rising and falling empires and cultures, Hebrew and Aramaic fell into disuse and were eventually replaced by Greek. Sometime around 250 B.C. someone decided to preserve those writings in a complete Greek translation of Hebrew Scripture.

**65. At least three or four centuries elapsed** between the close of the Old Testament writings and the opening of the New Testament. This silent period is called the intertestamental period and was comparable in length to the time that the judges ruled, or about the same number of years kings ruled Israel.

# 4

# The Missing Part—
# the Apocrypha

**66. The word *apocrypha*** originates from a Greek word that means "hidden." There are a number of books of Scripture that were not included in the Protestant Bible because their origins were not believed authentic. The apocrypha includes in particular the Old Testament books that are included in Roman Catholic versions of the Bible.

**67. The Greek word *apocrypha*** refers to a small group of ancient writings whose "divinely inspired" status has long been the subject of debate and controversy. Some of these books may have originally been written in Hebrew but were only known to exist in their Greek versions—one of the reasons the rabbis rejected them as part of Hebrew Scripture. They were included in the Septuagint, the Greek translation of the Hebrew Bible that was used by the early Christian church.

**68. The Apocrypha** was accepted as part of the Bible by Augustine in the late fourth century. Since much Roman Catholic theology is based on the writings of Augustine, Catholics accept the Apocrypha as part of the Word of God. However, neither the Jews nor Christians in Palestine ever accepted it as Scripture. Protestants during the Reformation rejected it as part of the Canon, and it does not appear in Protestant Bibles.

**69. Pseudepigrapha** is the term for the many other Old and New Testament apocryphal books that have been rejected and are considered of doubtful authenticity. The apocryphal books are considered those "hidden" books of the Old Testament that are found in Roman Catholic versions, but excluded from Protestant Bibles. The following books are included.

**70. First Esdras gives** the same historic account as the books of Chronicles, Ezra, and Nehemiah. An additional story is added in, called the "Debate of the Three Youths." The story is Persian and involves King Darius and Zerubbabel, a governor.

**71. Second Esdras** comes from a Hebrew source, but it has changed and expanded with various Christian additions. The book is also called "the Apocalypse of Ezra." The book explains seven different visions involving Ezra speaking on the people's behalf, salvation, Jerusalem and Rome, and a final vision concerning the sacred books Ezra is supposed to restore.

**72. Tobit** is a blind Jew in captivity in Nineveh. Tobit sends his son, Tobias, to collect a debt. Tobias falls in love with his cousin, Sara, along the way and has to defeat the demon Asmodeus in order to escape death unlike Sara's seven previous bridegrooms. Raphael helps him to do this. Tobias catches a fish in the Tigris River that eventually restores his father's sight.

**73. Judith** is a book about a beautiful Jewish widow of Bethulia. She plays the heroine of her book by saving her city from Nebuchadnezzar's forces. Beautiful Judith entices the general, Holofernes, into a drunken stupor after going to see him on the pretense of sharing military secrets. When he is asleep, she cuts off his head and brings it back to her city. The people pursue the fleeing enemy.

**74. Additions to Esther** may be more authentic than the other books as many scholars regard these passages as true additions to the original Hebrew. Some even consider the real Book of Esther an abbreviated work. The apocryphal version includes much of the same story line as the canonical Book of Esther.

**75. Wisdom of Solomon,** though named after the wisest man who ever lived, was not written by him or even about him. It is believed to have been composed originally in Greek, and there is evidence of Greek philosophy and Platonic terminology. It is a historical account of how the Jews have been helped by wisdom.

**76. Ecclesiasticus** was written around 180 B.C. and is held in high esteem by both Jews and early Christians. It contains the sayings of Joshua ben Sira, who recommended observing the law carefully and maintaining a healthy, pious fear of God. The book also gives practical advice for daily living.

**77. Baruch** may have more than one author, but it is likely that Baruch, a scribe of the prophet Jeremiah, was involved. The book offers encouragement to the Jews in light of their exile to Babylon. It serves as a historical guideline for that time period as well.

**78. Additions to Daniel** comes out of the Septuagint. The book includes stories regarding falsely accused people and an even more in-depth writing of the three Christians' prayers and praises from the fiery furnace. Daniel is a prominent figure in this apocryphal book.

**79. The Prayer of Manasseh** is just what the title says it is—King Manasseh's prayer to God while he was in captivity, as described in 2 Chronicles 13. God allowed him to be captured because he had worshiped idols and been an evil king. The book is thought to be Jewish in origin.

**80. First and Second Maccabees** trace Jewish history between 175 and 134 B.C. The books describe the hero Judas Maccabeus and his family, the Maccabees. The first book was translated from a Hebrew work in about 100 B.C. The second book is thought to have been taken from a work by Jason of Cyrene, a man little is known of. The first book is thought to be more accurate, though there are discrepancies between the two.

# 5

# The Bible into Translation

**81. The Vulgate** was written by Jerome (340–420) in A.D. 382. It was a translation in Latin from the original Old and New Testaments' original languages (Hebrew and Greek). The Vulgate has long been the Roman Catholic Church's authorized version.

**82. The Synod of Toulouse** in 1229 forbade everyone except priests from possessing a copy of the Scriptures. At that gathering Pope Gregory IX asked Dominican friars to question suspects and prosecute heretics, making the friars a powerful force and keeping the Bible out of the hands of laypeople.

**83. John Wycliffe (ca. 1328–1384)** was a reformer who wanted to make the Christian Scriptures accessible to common people. In the Middle Ages it was common for only officials in the church to be able to read or even have access to the Scriptures. Wycliffe's work is considered the most historically significant in the effort to make the Bible available to all people.

**84. The Wycliffe Bible** was translated from the Vulgate Bible into English by John Wycliffe in 1384. The Vulgate Bible was a Latin translation composed by Jerome. The Catholic church denounced Wycliffe as heretical for doing this as it was a forbidden act to translate the Bible into English at that time.

**85. The invention of movable type** by Johannes Gutenberg was recently hailed as the most important technical advancement of the last millennium. Gutenberg, a printer in Mainz, found a way to make many copies of a page by using letters made of lead. By 1456 he and his fellow printers had created nearly two hundred copies of Jerome's Vulgate Bible. Prior to that time, all books were hand printed on papyrus sheets or animal skin, making them expensive, time-intensive, and rare. Consequently, few people could read, and even fewer owned any books. Within twenty years of Gutenberg's first printed Bible, the printers of Mainz had created more Bibles than had been produced by hand in the previous fourteen hundred years.

**86. The printing press** not only allowed for the dissemination of the Scriptures but also for the spread of critical, sometimes satirical, examinations of the church's excesses. These writings fit the growing mood in Europe that the Roman church was out of touch with common people's lives.

**87. The first copy of the Gutenberg Bible** took three years of constant printing to complete. It was finished in 1455. It was done in two volumes, with 1,284 pages total. Nearly two hundred original Gutenberg Bibles were printed, and forty-eight still exist.

**88. William Tyndale** (ca. 1494–1536) believed the Bible should be read by everyone, not just the few who understood Latin, the language of the church. So he set out to translate the Bible into English.

**89. Accused of perverting the Scriptures,** Tyndale was forced to leave England, and his New Testament was burned as an "untrue translation." Arrested and imprisoned as a heretic, Tyndale was executed in Antwerp by strangling. His body was then burned at the stake in October 1536. William Tyndale is now honored as the "father of the English Bible." The Tyndale New Testament was published in

1526 from the ancient Hebrew and Greek texts. This version, too, was condemned by the church.

**90. An English Bible** was prepared by Miles Coverdale at the same time the Tyndale Bible was being written. The English Bible was published in 1535, though it was translated by a man who was not versed in Hebrew or Greek. Coverdale drew from the Vulgate, some early German versions, and partly from the Tyndale Bible. This was the first Bible that placed the Apocrypha in a separate section, under the title of "noncanonical."

**91. The Matthew Bible** was published in 1537 as an English Bible. It claimed to be "truly and purely translated into English by Thomas Matthew." In fact John Rogers wrote the Bible, which was a compilation of the English Bible and the Tyndale Bible.

**92. The Taverner Bible** was written just two years after Coverdale finished the English Bible. In reality it was only a revision of the Matthew Bible.

**93. The Great Bible** (1539) was the first widely popular English translation of the Scriptures to be owned and read by the common people. Produced by Miles Coverdale and John Rogers, it was based on translations from the Latin Vulgate, with additional notes from the writings of Martin Luther and Ulrich Zwingli. It was a significant improvement over the earlier Coverdale and Matthew Bibles due to its readability and understanding of poetry.

**94. The Geneva Bible** (1560) was a product of the Calvinist movement in northern Europe. Rather than simply relying on Roman Catholic translations, the English exiles in Geneva created prologues to each book of Scripture, added marginal notes to aid understanding, and spent considerable time recrafting the poetic elements of the various books. One outstanding feature that the translators developed was the numbering of chapters and verses—something that not only made it a popular Bible, but which has been copied by translators ever since.

**95. The Bishops' Bible** appeared in 1568 at the order of the Archbishop of Canterbury, Matthew Parker. The Geneva Bible was not given official endorsement by Queen Elizabeth. As a result a new edition was started shortly after the Geneva Bible was printed.

**96. The Rheims-Douay Version** was completed in 1610 by Roman Catholics who had escaped from England during Queen Elizabeth's reign. They settled in France and published the New Testament in Rheims in 1582 and the Old Testament in Douay in 1610. It is mainly a translation of the Latin Vulgate.

**97. While Gutenberg's Bible** was the first printed Bible, it was done in Latin, so was limited to a scholarly audience. But in 1522 the church in Spain produced the Complutensian Polyglot, the first Bible with the Old Testament in Hebrew and the New Testament in Greek.

**98. In 1603, James VI of Scotland** became King James I of England and began a program of peacemaking between hostile religious factions of Great Britain. That same year Dr. John Reynolds, the Puritan spokesman at a meeting of religious leaders at Hampton Court, proposed that a new English translation of the Bible be issued in honor of the new king. The 1768 revision is what most people now know as the King James Bible.

**99. The King James Bible,** which was originally named the Authorized Version, was first suggested by the Puritans in 1604. James, who disagreed with the Calvinist leanings of the Geneva Bible, wanted a version that supported the right of kings to rule over people. He appointed fifty-four scholars, divided into eight teams, and demanded they examine all earlier English versions to aid in translation. Produced in 1611, the translation is marked by beautiful language, an accurate translation, and modesty when faced with embarrassing language and situations.

**100. The first Native American translation** of the Bible, completed in 1663, was made into the language of the Algonquin tribe, whom the Puritan colonists then promptly wiped out.

**101. Stephen Langton,** who was archbishop of Canterbury in the thirteenth century, created chapter divisions for the Bible. He died in 1228, and his work remains visible in the Bibles of today.

**102. The Aitken Bible** was the first Bible printed in the United States. Congress authorized its publishing in 1781.

**103. The Revised Version** was begun in 1870 in order to update the King James Version. The effort included both English scholars as well as American ones, and also included various denominations of believers. The English version was completed in 1885.

**104. The American Standard Version** grew out of the Revised Version, which was worked on by Americans and the English. The English advisors had the decisive vote on differences in translation. The Americans agreed not to publish any editions for fourteen years. After that time period was over, the American Revision Committee produced an edition with the American preferences in 1901.

**105. The Red Letter Bible** first appeared in 1928, when an American printer decided to put the direct quotations of Jesus in red ink. The idea caught on, particularly with Catholic printers, who still rely on red letters to note things of importance. The practice led directly to the phrase "red-letter day" to denote an important day in someone's life.

**106. The Revised Standard Version** came out in 1952 and deserves mention because it was a modernization of the King James Version using current biblical scholarship to determine the underlying Greek and Hebrew texts.

**107. The Jerusalem Bible** (1966), popular among Roman Catholics, contains about a dozen books that Jews and Protestants don't consider part of the Holy Scriptures.

**108. The Good News Bible** of 1976 became a best-selling version quickly and remains a popular modern version throughout churches today.

**109. The New International Bible** came out in 1978 and remains one of the most popular versions used today.

**110. There are complete Bibles in more than forty European languages** and 125 Asian and Pacific Island languages. There are also Bible translations in more than one hundred African languages, with another five hundred African-language versions of some portion of the Bible. At least fifteen complete Native American Bibles have been produced.

# 6

# Funny and
# Fresh Takes

**111. The Gothic Bible** did not contain the books of 1 Kings or 2 Kings. The reason was that Ulfilas, the missionary who brought the gospel to the Goths of northern Europe in the mid–300s, didn't think the war-loving Gothic people should be reading about all the wars perpetrated by the Jewish kings. It's important to note, however, that the Goths had no written language at the time. In translating the Bible into the Gothic language, Ulfilas invented a Gothic alphabet so that the people could read the Good News for themselves.

**112. The Bug Bible** was published in 1535 and was known more by its real name, the Coverdale Bible. It was dubbed the "Bug Bible" because of its rendering of Psalm 91:5: "Thou shalt not need to be afrayd for eny bugges by night."

**113. The Breeches Bible,** or the Geneva Bible as it was better known, appeared in 1560. Genesis 3:7 reads that Adam and Eve "sowed figge-tree leaves together and made themselves breeches."

**114. The Placemakers Bible** was the 1562 edition of the Geneva Bible. The word "peacemakers" in Matthew 5:9 was changed to "placemakers" to read: "Blessed are the placemakers."

**115. The Tryacle Bible** came out in 1568 and was officially called the Bishops' Bible. The word "tryacle" was used in place of the word "balm" in Jeremiah. One instance can be found in Jeremiah 8:22: "Is there no tryacle in Gilead?" (*Tryacle* is a bit of a double entendre. It means "an antidote to poison," "a sweet dessert," and is sometimes used as a perjorative for anything cloyingly sweet.)

**116. The King James Version** (first edition) was completed by Robert Barker, the official printer of King James I, as early as 1611. Scholars call this a "He" Bible because it renders Ruth 3:15 as ". . . He went into the city" instead of ". . . She went into the city." Different copies of the KJV published between 1611 and 1614 contain either he or she, indicating that two presses were producing the Bible at that time. Later editions accepted "she" as the proper wording.

**117. The Wicked Bible,** or Adulterous Bible, was printed in 1632. The word "not" was accidentally left out of the seventh commandment: "You shall commit adultery" (Exod. 20:14).

**118. The Unrighteous Bible** was the Cambridge edition of 1653. The word "not" was left out of 1 Corinthians 6:9, which made it appear as: "The unrighteous shall inherit the kingdom of God." Another mistake from this version was found in Romans 6:13—the word "righteousness" was substituted for "unrighteousness"—"Neither yield ye your members as instruments of righteousness unto sin."

**119. The Vinegar Bible** was an Oxford edition from 1717. The heading for the segment of Luke 20 now known as the "parable of the tenants" was known in editions of that time period as "the parable of the vineyard." The word *vinegar* was mistakenly used in place of *vineyard*.

**120. The Printers' Bible** came out in the early eighteenth century, but an exact date is unknown. Psalm 119:161 reads, "printers have persecuted me without cause." The word *printers* should read as *princes.*

**121. The Murderers' Bible** was printed in 1801. The word *murmurers* was replaced with *murderers* in Jude 16: "These are murderers, complainers. . . ."

**122. The To Remain Bible** was printed in Cambridge in 1805. A well-meaning proofreader was unsure about a comma in the manuscript and queried it. The editor penciled in the words "to remain"; thus Galatians 4:29 reads "he that was born after the flesh persecuted him that was born after the spirit *to remain,* even so it is now."

**123. The Standing Fishes Bible** was printed in 1806, and mistakenly used the word *fishes* for *fishers* in Ezekiel 47:10: "And it shall come to pass that the fishes shall stand on it."

**124. The Discharge Bible** also appeared in 1806. In 1 Timothy 5:21, the apostle says, "I discharge thee . . . that thou observe these things." The correct wording would have been "I charge thee . . ."

**125. The Idle Shepherd Bible** appeared in 1809. This edition mistook the "idol shepherd" of Zechariah 11:17 and made it read "idle shepherd."

**126. The Ears to Ear Bible** was published in 1810. Matthew 13:43 reads, "Who hath ears to ear, let him hear" instead of "Who hath ears to hear, let him hear."

**127. The Wife-hater Bible** was printed in 1810. The word "life" was changed to "wife" in Luke 14:26: "If any man comes to me, and hates not his father . . . and his own wife also. . . ." It should read, "If any man comes to me, and hates not his father . . . and his own life also. . . ."

**128. Rebekah's Camels Bible** is an 1823 edition that gives Rebekah "camels" instead of "damsels" in Genesis 24:61: "Rebekah arose, and her camels . . ."

# 7

# Famous Words
# and Phrases

**129. "Raising Cain"** means to act with abandonment or wildly. As a phrase, it is most likely descended from the Genesis character Cain who killed his brother, Abel, and was forever marked as a violent man.

**130. "Jezebel" or "Delilah"** is the name often given to a woman of cunning and deceit. Both Bible characters were beautiful, though calculating in nature. Delilah was a seductress; Jezebel was a queen.

**131. A "Judas"** can only refer to one personality trait: betrayal. Judas Iscariot betrayed his relationship to the Lord for thirty pieces of silver.

**132. "Doubting Thomas"** didn't believe Jesus had truly risen from the dead. He insisted on touching the nail marks in the Lord's hands and side before he would believe. Today we call a person with doubts a doubting Thomas.

**133. "Jonah"** is considered an unlucky name. The prophet Jonah tried unsuccessfully to run from God's calling. He took refuge on a boat and brought nothing but trouble to the other passengers, because God would not forget Jonah. Someone who brings bad luck or misfortune is considered a Jonah.

**134. The word** *beautiful* was first used in the English language by William Tyndale when he produced his English translation of the New Testament in 1526. Some scholars considered it an outrage that a translator would use a new, fashionable word in his interpretation of Scripture.

**135. "The salt of the earth."** Many of the words we use in our culture come from the Lord Jesus. In describing his disciples with these words in Matthew 5:13, Christ was saying that they were valuable—salt being the preferred method of payment in those days. The phrase is still used to describe people we find valuable or important.

**136. "Seek and ye shall find."** These oft-quoted words of Jesus come from his Sermon on the Mount in Matthew 7:7. It is still generally used as advice or encouragement to those who need to be seeking.

**137. "A wolf in sheep's clothing."** Jesus created this phrase in Matthew 7:15 to describe religious leaders who appear righteous on the outside but are actually evil on the inside. We still use it to describe hypocrites or those who portray goodness while intending evil.

**138. "The faith to move mountains."** Although not currently used quite as often as it was in the twentieth century, the phrase refers to the power of belief. The words were first said by the Lord Jesus in Matthew 17:20 when he was talking to his disciples about healing the sick and the demon possessed.

**139. "The blind leading the blind."** Jesus coined this phrase in Matthew 15:14 when describing false teachers who insist they know the truth but do not, therefore leading innocent people astray. In our culture we generally use it as a negative descriptor for the self-important and self-deluded.

**140. "Do not throw pearls before swine."** Jesus' words in Matthew 7:6 urge believers to take care with their message; it is not necessary to teach to those who are openly hostile to the gospel. A person wouldn't throw precious pearls to pigs, and Christians shouldn't throw the gift of salvation to those who will only turn around and attack them.

**141. "Eat, drink, and be merry"** was a phrase created by Jesus in Luke 12 while telling a cautionary tale about a rich fool who thought the rest of his life was set. The fool died that very night. The words are still generally used in the sarcastic or pejorative sense.

**142. "The straight and narrow."** Following the small, less-traveled path leads to the narrow gate of life. In Matthew 7:14, Jesus cautioned his followers against following the more glamorous, broad, and well-traveled path that led to a wide gate full of destruction.

**143. "A good Samaritan."** Someone who goes out of the way to help another can be likened to the famed character of Jesus' parable in Luke 10:30–37. The hero acts for the good of another with no thought to his own situation.

**144. "Sweating blood"** is a phrase used to describe someone going through a very difficult time. The etymology of the word relates back to Luke 22:44, when Christ's anguish in the Garden of Gethsemane caused him to sweat blood—something physicians say is, in fact, possible for those enduring great duress.

**145. "The forbidden fruit"** is one of many Old Testament phrases still used regularly in the English language. The original "forbidden fruit" was the fruit from the tree of the knowledge of good and evil. Adam and Eve were instructed to stay away from it in Genesis 2:17, but when the Serpent tempted them to eat of it, the couple disobeyed God and chose to sin. Now we use the phrase to refer to partaking in an activity we know to be wrong or sensual.

**146. "Fire and brimstone"** were the tools God used to destroy the cities of Sodom and Gomorrah, according to Genesis 19:24.

The apostle John used those same words to describe the ultimate end of Satan in Revelation 21:8. Due to its colorful imagery, the phrase is generally used to describe preachers who focus on the punishment aspects of the biblical story, or for any fiery speaker who makes reference to a bad end for wrongdoers.

**147. "Taking a sabbatical"** comes from the old Jewish notion of "taking time off." Leviticus 25 commands the people to allow the ground to lie fallow every seventh year in order to refresh itself—an action that was referred to as the "sabbatical year."

**148. "An eye for an eye"** is a phrase that first appears in Leviticus 24:20. Rather than being a vindictive call for revenge, it actually limited the damage one person could do to another when taking retribution. Human nature encourages an individual to hurt others, but the Old Testament law wanted to limit that hurt to equivalent damage.

**149. "A land flowing with milk and honey"** were the words God used to describe Palestine to Moses in Exodus 3:8. It's now generally used to describe a fine or pleasant place.

**150. "The apple of my eye"** is a phrase first created in Deuteronomy 32:10 to describe God's perspective of Israel. The Hebrew words literally mean "center" or "pupil" of the eye, but in the poetic sense they refer to someone or something highly valued by another. The poet David asks God in Psalm 17:8, "Keep me as the apple of your eye."

**151. "Scapegoat."** On the Day of Atonement, the high priest would lay his hands on one goat, symbolically transferring the sins of the people onto it. However, instead of being killed, that goat was driven into the wilderness as a symbol of the sins being "gone." The goat, which took the blame for the sins of others, was known as the "scapegoat."

**152. "Spare the rod and spoil the child."** This bit of homely wisdom (generally quoted by senior citizens when somebody else's kids are acting up) is based on the wisdom of King Solomon, who says in Proverbs 13:24 that a parent "who spares the rod hates his son."

**153. "Pride goes before a fall,"** one of the most commonly quoted phrases in American history, were the words of King Solomon in Proverbs 16:18, referring to the fact that a prideful attitude can blind us and lead us into trouble.

**154. "A fly in the ointment"** is a phrase commonly used to describe something that has gone wrong with a system or procedure. It comes from Ecclesiastes 10:1, which states that "dead flies spoil the perfumer's ointment."

**155. "Woe is me!"** This phrase, once common in nineteenth-century literature, was first used in Isaiah 6:5 when the prophet came face-to-face with God. It also appears in the Book of Jeremiah as an expression of sorrow.

**156. "A drop in the bucket."** Generally used to refer to "a small amount" or "a meaningless portion," the words are lifted in their entirety from Isaiah 40:15, in which we are told that to the Lord "the nations are a drop in the bucket."

**157. "Holier than thou."** These words, which in our modern culture are generally used to describe a self-righteous person, were used in that same sense by the Lord in Isaiah 65:5 to criticize those who felt themselves better than others.

**158. "Like a lamb to the slaughter"** were words first used in Isaiah 53:7 to describe the coming Messiah's willingness to accept his fate. It's now generally used in reference to an innocent victim or someone who is bound to lose in his or her circumstances.

**159. "The skin of our teeth."** Generally used to mean "just barely," the imagery comes from Job 19:20. The phrase was popularized when made the title of a wildly successful play by American playwright Thornton Wilder.

**160. "Can a leopard change its spots?"** This rhetorical question, which suggests people cannot change what they are inherently, was coined by the prophet Jeremiah in 13:23 of his book.

**161. "Feet of clay,"** an expression which has come to mean a personal flaw in an individual, was first used by the prophet Daniel when describing the statue he had seen in King Nebuchadnezzar's dream. The feet of the statue were made of clay mixed with iron—a weak base for such a big, heavy monument.

**162. "The handwriting on the wall"** is a phrase that comes from Daniel chapter 5. The carnal King Belshazzar had seen a hand appear and write a mysterious message. Calling upon Daniel to interpret the message, the king learned that God had weighed Belshazzar on an eternal scale and found him wanting. His kingdom was to be taken away that very night—leading to our use of the phrase as "something inevitable that we can all see happening."

**163. "We reap what we sow."** Generally accepted as cultural wisdom that means "you get what you earn," the phrase is lifted from Paul's letter to the Galatians in chapter 6, verse 7.

**164. "The powers that be,"** a phrase first created by Bible translator William Tyndale, is usually used to refer to "the government" or "those in charge." It means those in positions of authority are there by God's choice and therefore exist only because he wishes them to. The phrase was used by the apostle Paul in Romans 13:1 when, as the King James Version reads, he noted, "the powers that be are ordained of God."

**165. "A thorn in the side."** The apostle Paul first used this phrase in 2 Corinthians 12:7 to describe some sort of physical ailment. Though he pleaded with God to take it away, the problem continued, thus keeping Paul humble. We still use the phrase to refer to an ongoing problem.

**166. "Money is the root of all evil."** This popular phrase is actually a bit of a mistranslation from 1 Timothy 6:10. The actual words of Paul stated that "the *love* of money is the root of all kinds of evil" (emphasis added). Still the fact remains that lusting after money can get us into all sorts of trouble.

**167. "Nothing new under the sun."** This statement by Solomon demonstrates the author's realization that despite temporary changes from one day to the next, there is nothing truly new or unexpected under the rising and falling of the sun each day. The phrase comes from Ecclesiastes 1:9.

**168. "The fat of the land."** Pharaoh spoke these words to Joseph in Genesis 45:18. Joseph was to pass them on in turn to his brothers, who were hungry and in need of a place to live due to the famine affecting the land of Israel. The Egyptian king promised Joseph the best land of Egypt and that he and his brothers would be well provided for and able to eat "the fat of the land."

**169. "All things to all men."** Paul is speaking in 1 Corinthians 9:22 of how he has become all things to everyone in order to win some to Christ. The phrase now is often seen as a "sell-out" point, as it is difficult to be everything to everyone and keep sight of one's own welfare.

# 8

# Strange and Amazing Facts

**170. A stack of scrolls** was the form of the Bible until the fourth century A.D. Then it was compiled into one volume, though it was hardly complete at that point!

**171. It wasn't until the sixteenth century,** many, many years after the Bible was first printed, that it was divided into the chapters and verses we are accustomed to today.

**172. No mention!** There are two books of the Bible that never state the name of God: Esther and Song of Solomon.

**173. There are twenty-four books** in the Hebrew Bible. Generally the books are categorized within three sections: the Law

(Torah), Prophets, and Writings. The Hebrew Bible has only what Protestants would call the "Old Testament."

**174. The Protestant version** of the Old Testament contains thirty-nine books. This is different from both the Hebrew Bible and the Catholic Bible. The New Testament of the Protestant version contains twenty-seven books.

**175. The Catholic Bible's Old Testament** contains the thirty-nine books of the Protestant version's Old Testament but also includes seven books of the Apocrypha.

**176. How many chapters?** There are 929 chapters in the Old Testament and 260 in the New Testament, making a grand total of 1,189 chapters in all!

**177. How many letters?** With 3,566,480 letters in the Bible, and a word count between 773,692 and 773,746, depending on how the hyphenated words are counted, this book is quite large.

**178. The shortest book** in the New Testament is 3 John, which contains only 294 words in its fourteen verses! John's second book has one less verse but four more words.

**179. The shortest book** in the Old Testament is Obadiah.

**180. The longest book** in the Bible is the Book of Psalms. It has 150 psalms.

**181. The longest verse in the Bible** (King James Version) is Esther 8:9, which has ninety words total. The shortest verse, John 11:35, includes only two words: "Jesus wept."

**182. The Book of Isaiah** is the most-often quoted Old Testament book, with 419 references made to it in the New Testament. The Book of Psalms is second and referred to in the New Testament 414 times.

**183. The oldest verses in the Bible** are believed to be fragments from "the Song of Deborah."

**184. The newest verses in the Bible** are thought to be found in the Gospel of John, which dates from around A.D. 100.

**185. Job was written when?** Job, the book that appears before the Psalms, is actually a much older book than the books it is located near. Job and Genesis are actually on similar timelines!

**186. The most press?** David receives second place for being mentioned a whopping 1,118 times in the Bible. He is second only to Jesus in this regard. Sarah, the wife of Abraham, receives the most references as a woman—fifty-six!

**187. The name *Jesus*** appears seven hundred times in the Gospels and Acts, and less than seventy times in the Epistles. The name *Christ* can be found sixty times throughout the Gospels and Acts, but 240 times in the Epistles and the Book of Revelation.

**188. The most press for an animal?** Sheep win the prize with mention of this very necessary animal occurring over four hundred different times.

**189. Who was the oldest?** Methuselah is believed to have lived 969 years on earth before he died (Gen. 5:27), making him the longest-lived person. Prior to the flood, people lived very long lives, but afterward, only a few (the patriarchs and Moses among them) lived beyond the expected seventy- or eighty-year life span.

**190. The longest-reigning king** in the Bible was Manasseh, who oversaw the kingdom of Judah for fifty-five years (2 Kings 21:1). The shortest-reigning king was Zimri, who wore the crown of Israel for only seven days (1 Kings 16:15).

**191. Weddings galore.** King Solomon, the son of David, is the most-often married man in the whole Bible. This king had seven hundred wives (all of royal birth!) along with an additional three hundred concubines (1 Kings 11:3).

**192. A longer name** can't be found in the Bible than that of Maher-shalal-hash-baz. The Lord told Isaiah, in 8:3, to give his child, born of a prophetess, this name, which means "quick to the plunder, swift to the spoil."

**193. Though God is invisible and has no body parts,** the Bible always refers to him with masculine pronouns, and we are said to be made "in his image" according to Genesis.

**194. Shakespeare honored?!** William Shakespeare is perhaps the only man not of Bible times who is honored in the Bible. How? In honor of his forty-sixth birthday, which happened to be the year the King James Version was being printed for the first time, the scholars took the forty-sixth psalm and made sure that forty-six words into the psalm appeared the word *shake* and forty-six words from the end of the psalm appeared the word *spear.*

# 9

# Famous Quotes

**195.** "**The book of books,** the storehouse and magazine of life and comfort, the holy Scriptures."—George Herbert

**196.** "**Prosperity is the blessing of the Old Testament,** adversity is the blessing of the New."—Francis Bacon

**197.** "**Most people are bothered** by those passages in Scripture which they cannot understand; but as for me . . . the passages which trouble me most are those that I do understand."—Mark Twain

**198.** "**The English Bible,** a book which, if everything else in our language should perish, would alone suffice to show the whole extent of its beauty and power."—Thomas Babington Macaulay

**199.** "**The Bible is a window** in this prison of hope, through which we look into eternity."—John Sullivan Dwight

**200.** "**If you believe those four words,** 'In the beginning God,' you have no problem believing all of the Bible."—Raymond Barber

**201.** **"Unless I am convicted of error** by the testimony of Scripture or by manifest reasoning, I stand convicted by the Scriptures to which I have appealed, and my conscience is taken captive by God's word."—Martin Luther

**202.** **"A young man who wishes** to remain a sound Atheist cannot be too careful of his reading. There are traps everywhere—'Bibles laid open, millions of surprises'— . . . God is, if I may say it, very unscrupulous."—C. S. Lewis

**203.** **"Either the Bible will keep you away from sin,** or sin will keep you away from the Bible!"—Author Unknown

**204.** **"The Bible is literature, not dogma."**—George Santayana

**205.** **"The Bible is no mere book,** but a living creature, with a power that conquers all that oppose it."—Napoleon Bonaparte

**206.** **"In the twentieth century our highest praise** has been to call the Bible 'the world's best-seller.' And it has come to be more and more difficult to say whether we think it is a best-seller because it is great, or vice versa."—Daniel Boorstin

**207.** **"There are no songs comparable to the songs of Zion,** no orations equal to those of the prophets, and no politics like those which the Scriptures teach."—John Milton

**208.** **"When you read God's Word,** you must constantly be saying to yourself, it is talking to me, and about me."—Søren Kierkegaard

**209.** **"You can learn more about human nature** by reading the Bible than by living in New York."—William Lyon Phelps

**210.** **"The New Testament is the very best book** that ever was or ever will be known in the world."—Charles Dickens

**211.** **"What you bring away from the Bible** depends to some extent on what you carry to it."—Oliver Wendell Holmes

**212.** **"The Bible is alive,** it speaks to me; it has feet, it runs after me; it has hands, it lays hold on me."—Martin Luther

**213.** **"The Bible tells us to love our neighbors,** and also to love our enemies; probably because they are generally the same people."—G. K. Chesterton

**214.** **"Intense study of the Bible** will keep any man from being vulgar in point of style."—Samuel Taylor Coleridge

**215.** **"'The Bible,' we are told sometimes, 'gives us such a beautiful picture of what we should be.'** Nonsense! It gives us no picture at all. It reveals to us a fact: It tells us what we really are; it says, This is the form in which God created you, to which He has restored you; this is the work which the Eternal Son, the God of Truth and Love, is continually carrying on within you."—F. D. Maurice

**216.** **"Read the whole Bible, and read it in order;** two chapters in the Old Testament and one in the New, daily if you can possibly spare the time; and you will have more time than you are aware of; if you retrench all needless visits, and save the hours spent in useless or unimportant conversation."—Adam Clarke, a Methodist circuit preacher of the nineteenth century, believed that only through regular Bible reading would Christians grow wise in their salvation.

**217.** **"You may as well quit reading** and hearing the Word of God, and give in to the devil, if you do not desire to live according to it."—Martin Luther

# Part II

# The *Whole* Story

# 10

# The Old Testament Books

**218. The Books of Moses.** Otherwise known as the Pentateuch, the first five books of the Bible attributed to Moses are the cornerstone of the books contributed by later generations. These books include Genesis, Exodus, Leviticus, Numbers, and Deuteronomy.

**219. Genesis.** *Genesis* comes from a word meaning "to be born." From that same word we also get words like *genetic, congenital,* and *genealogy.* Though it marks the beginning, the best way to look at Genesis is not merely to begin and look forward, but to stand at Exodus and look back. Moses is writing for his fellow Israelite slaves. As they struggle with Egypt's oppression, Moses answers the question, "How did we get in this mess?" Genesis is the answer to that question. It tells the story of the Israelites' ancestors—all the way back to the first human beings.

**220. Exodus.** This book opens several hundred years after the close of Genesis. Jacob and some seventy family members had grown into hundreds of thousands. God's promise of descendants to Abraham also included a promise of land on which the descendants would live. This land had already been settled and was called Canaan, after its original settlers. It is now the area of Palestine or Israel. *Exodus* means "the going out of." It is the story of the Hebrew people being led by Moses out of Egyptian captivity into the wilderness for forty years.

**221. Leviticus.** The Levites were descended from Jacob's son Levi. Moses and Aaron were Levites. The Levites were to keep the tabernacle and all its services for the rest of the nation, and the priests were to have the most essential parts of that service. This book is somewhat of an appendix to Exodus as it is a log of the laws and guidelines for the Israelites.

**222. Numbers.** The English title of this book refers to the census of the twelve tribes that opens the book. The Hebrew title, Ba-Midbar ("in the wilderness"), is more accurately descriptive because the book begins with the decision to leave Sinai and cross the desert toward the Promised Land.

**223. Deuteronomy.** This book is essentially Moses' farewell address—actually three addresses—in which he restates the acts of God. Solemnly Moses warns of the temptations of Canaan and its evil ways. Moses pleads for loyalty to and love of God as the main condition for life in the Promised Land. A central message in Deuteronomy is that the worship of God is to be centralized in one place, so that the paganism of local shrines may be eliminated.

**224. The books of history.** If the books of Moses can be considered the cornerstone of the Bible, then the next twelve books can be thought of as the first story of the building. The historical record of ancient Israel that began with Genesis through Deuteronomy is continued with these next twelve books. While the first five books brought Israel to the edge of the Promised Land, these next twelve tell what happened once Israel took up residence there.

**225. Joshua.** Moses and Aaron were not allowed to enter the Promised Land, and neither were any of the people who came out of Egypt because of the Israelites' griping in the wilderness. Permission came at last for the Israelites to "conquer" the Promised Land after forty years of waiting. The Book of Joshua tells this story. As in many war stories, it gets pretty gory.

**226. Judges** recounts the history of Israel from the death of Joshua to the time just before the birth of the Hebrew prophet Samuel, roughly a two-hundred-year span. The judges were warrior-like rulers over the tribes of Israel.

**227. Ruth.** The short Book of Ruth—shortest of all the historical books—provides a welcome respite from the harsh times described at the end of Judges. The opening verses tell of the Moabites, Ruth's marriage to a Hebrew man during a time of famine, and how she chose to return to Judah with her mother-in-law after her husband's death. Her loyalty and kindness were rewarded and forever remembered by the Jewish people because she became the great-grandmother of King David.

**228. 1 and 2 Samuel and 1 and 2 Kings.** Originally the two books of Samuel and the two books of Kings were each a single book in the Hebrew Canon of the Bible, telling the history of the kingdom of Israel. Once they were translated into Greek in the Septuagint, they no longer fit on single scrolls and were expanded into four books. Samuel contains the history of the prophet Samuel—the last judge of Israel—and the stormy tale of Israel's first two kings, Saul and David.

**229. The division of Kings** occurred when the Book of Samuel was divided into 1 Samuel and 2 Samuel, the Book of Kings was divided into 1 Kings and 2 Kings, and the Book of Chronicles was divided into 1 Chronicles and 2 Chronicles. The motivation was not spiritual but practical—the books were simply too long to keep on one scroll.

**230. 1 and 2 Chronicles** is the ancient *Reader's Digest* version of everything that had already taken place in the Bible from Genesis forward. It is abridged and simplified, with many of the nasty parts taken out. The first nine chapters contain long tables of "begats," showing the descendants of the Hebrew tribes, from Adam through the time of King David. The rest of 1 Chronicles and most of 2 Chronicles deal with the reigns of David and Solomon and the subsequent history of the kingdom of Judah until the Babylonian exile. Since these books are placed last in the Hebrew Canon, the Hebrew Scriptures end on a liberating note, with echoes of the Exodus.

**231. Ezra** opens with a decree of Cyrus, the king of Persia, following his capture of Babylon in 539 B.C., that those who want to may leave Babylon and return to Jerusalem to rebuild the temple. Founder of an extensive empire that lasted more than two hundred years, Cyrus was an extraordinary leader. Under Cyrus and his successors, much of the ancient Near East, from India to Egypt and the border of Greece, was brought under one ruler. Unlike other ancient conquerors who enforced their own religions on conquered peoples, Cyrus permitted the captive nations to preserve and restore their own institutions.

**232. Nehemiah.** Jerusalem was constantly raided by various marauders. Nehemiah's particular concern was the security of Jerusalem, so he returned from exile specifically to help. He organized the people and rebuilt the city walls in fifty-five days. While Ezra's role was that of a priest, Nehemiah's was that of governor. When the rebuilding was completed, Ezra was invited to rededicate the city by reading from the book of Moses. Ezra-Nehemiah make a distinctive pair of books, together recording the rebuilding of Jerusalem after the exile.

**233. Esther (Hadassah in Hebrew).** While Ezra-Nehemiah deal with events in Jerusalem, Esther tells of events far away. As Ruth was a vignette sketched in the period of the judges, Esther is a vignette sketched in the time of the exile. As one of the exiles, Esther finds herself in the service of the king of Persia. The king sets out to select a new queen, and the beautiful Jewish woman, Esther, is chosen. Haman, the king's right-hand man, plans to rid his country of the Jews. Through a fascinating sequence of events involving Esther, Haman's rampage against the Jews backfires. Esther retains the favor of the king and the Jewish people are saved.

**234. The books of poetry.** Job, Psalms, Proverbs, Ecclesiastes, and Song of Solomon make up the Bible's books of poetry. Hebrew poetry is picturesque and vivid. There is a rhythm or cadence to Hebrew poetry that is lost to some degree in the translation. It is filled with concrete images and deep emotion. It touches the soul.

The books of poetry aren't just a change in style from previous books; the subject matter shifts as well. Wisdom takes center stage in these five books; therefore, they are called the "wisdom literature" of the Bible.

**235. Job.** Whenever the troubling question "Why do bad things happen to good people?" comes up, Job is first to come to mind. But few people ever really tackle this book that reads like the script for a play. The central characters are Job, three of his friends, a bystander, and God. The supporting cast includes Job's wife and children, the angels, and Satan as chief of the angels. The first two chapters and the last two chapters are prose, and the thirty-nine chapters in between consist of poetic dialogue between the central characters.

**236. Psalms.** While Jews and Christians share the entire Hebrew Scriptures, or Old Testament, Psalms is the most emotionally and intensely shared book of Hebrew Scripture. Jews know many of the psalms and individual verses by heart. Jesus often quoted or referred to the Psalms. Martin Luther called the Book of Psalms "a Bible in Miniature." The 150 "rosaries" later instituted by the Roman Catholic Church are in honor of the 150 psalms.

**237. Proverbs.** Some proverbs are strung together in a meaningful sequence, while others are independent of each other and need to be "unpacked" by the reader. The opening chapters of Proverbs carry extended proverbs that progress with each verse. And mostly one-liner bits of wisdom form chapters ten and following. Proverbs leaves no ambiguity over the contrast between the righteous and the wicked.

**238. Ecclesiastes.** If Job reads like a play, and Psalms like poetry, and Proverbs like a book of maxims, then Ecclesiastes reads like an essay, or the thoughts of an old man thinking out loud. Its subject is the vanity of life. The book approaches Job's question, but from the opposite side: If this universe is governed by a moral God, why doesn't everything make sense? The conclusion of this book's search is that regardless of any apparent vanity, fearing God and keeping his commandments is the wisest course of action.

**239. Song of Solomon.** Plain and simple, this book is an erotic love poem. The writing resembles Egyptian love poetry and Arabic wedding songs that praise the charm and beauty of the bride. The traditional interpretation, both in Judaism and Christianity, is that these love poems represent Yahweh's love for Israel while also establishing God's high regard for male-female love and sexuality.

**240. Isaiah** opens by dating himself according to the reign of a particular king in Israel's history and then describing his visions in the form of poetry. Throughout his book, Isaiah made key references to historical markers, which keep his writings in context with the historical books. The other prophets often followed this form. Isaiah's ministry spread over the reigns of four of Judah's kings. Isaiah is quoted in the New Testament more often than any other book of prophecy.

**241. Jeremiah** was another firebrand prophet of the declining years of Judah. Jeremiah, whose name meant "God hurled," was born in a tiny village northeast of Jerusalem, and before long, perhaps while he was still in his teens, he was thrown into the midst of his nation's most terrifying crisis. He was a faithful prophet to God but unpopular among the people. The young Jeremiah declared that the Babylonians would destroy the nation because the children of Israel had forgotten their God.

**242. Lamentations** is a brief book of sorrowful poems, some in the form of alphabetic acrostics, which recall the grim fate of Jerusalem following its destruction by the Babylonians in 587/6 B.C. The title is derived from the Hebrew word *qinoth* ("dirges" or "laments"). In Christian Old Testaments, the book is placed after Jeremiah, but it is found in the third part of the Hebrew Canon Writings. The poems are bitterly sad elegies for the "dead" city, but they express hope that God will restore a humbled and repentant Israel.

**243. Ezekiel** is one of the hardest books to read in the Bible. It is long, with a somber tone like Jeremiah. Its images are complex and hard to understand. Babylon besieged Israel before the capital, Jerusalem, finally fell. During those years of siege, captives were taken from the land and shipped to Babylon. Ezekiel was one of the captives. Ezekiel dealt first with the problems that caused Israel to lose her land. Second, he wanted his people to maintain hope for the future.

**244. Daniel.** Like Ezekiel, the Book of Daniel has some complicated images. These images add to the glorious picture of the future of Israel. The central figure in that future was the Messiah, the Jews' image of hope. The first half of the book is straightforward narrative and is the source of some of the Bible's most loved stories: Shadrach, Meshach, and Abednego in the fiery furnace; Daniel in the lion's den; and the story that gave rise to the saying, "You could see the handwriting on the wall."

**245. Hosea** is a prophet of love. Hosea's own experiences with his wayward wife, Gomer, are used as a symbol to illustrate God's pain in dealing with Israel. Like Gomer's sin, Israel's sin would be punished before there could be restoration. In the Book of Hosea, the sins of Israel are spelled out, and she is described as a "harlot." God is portrayed as a faithful and loving husband and Israel as an adulterous wife.

**246. Joel's** theme is "This is the day of the Lord." The day of the Lord shows up in other prophetic books as well and means a day of reckoning—a day of judgment. It refers to a time when God brings down the wicked and haughty and lifts up the humble. The day of the Lord meant destruction for some and deliverance for others. Joel spoke of a day of the Lord approaching for Israel by describing a ravaging plague of locusts.

**247. Amos** prophesied at about the same time as Hosea and Joel. Amos was a sheepherder from a Judean village who left his flocks to denounce the sins of his people during the time of the northern King Jeroboam II (786–744 B.C.), a prosperous time in Israel. Though a herdsman, Amos used some of the purest and most classical Hebrew in the entire Old Testament. In a style of informal satire, Amos attacked the oppression of the poor by the rich, as well as the latter's empty piety and immoral religious practices. If the people did not mend their corrupt ways, Amos warned, they would be destroyed.

**248. Obadiah** is the shortest book in the Old Testament—only one chapter. Like Joel, he emphasized the coming day of the Lord. He said that since all nations have a day of reckoning, it does not pay to gloat when another nation encounters misfortune. He also emphasized the often-used words of wisdom, "As you have done it, so it will be done to you."

**249. Jonah.** This book marks a distinct change of pace. Jonah's story is told in narrative form about how he first refused to deliver a message of warning to the great city of Nineveh, capital of Assyria. Israel's prophets often had words to deliver to surrounding nations, but Jonah had no desire to deliver a message of repentance to the enemies of his people. Jonah attempted to run away, booking passage on a ship going to Tarshish in southern Spain, the farthest-known earthly point to which a man could then travel. In the end Jonah learned a great lesson in the depth of God's mercy.

**250. Micah** returns to the normal poetic style of the prophets. His writings are structured in three stages: reproof, threat, and promise. Micah reminded the people of all that God had done for them in the past. He called them to obedience in the present and hopefulness for the future. He spoke to both the people of the Northern Kingdom and the Southern Kingdom.

**251. Nahum.** Like Jonah, Nahum was concerned with the city of Nineveh. Here there is no narrative story, but where Jonah gave us just the overview, Nahum spells out the full indictment of the city's wrongdoings. Descriptive words are piled on one another, creating rapidly moving pictures. Nahum lived long after Jonah. Nineveh's embrace of morality had ended, and Nahum warned them of their final fall.

**252. Habakkuk** foresaw the assault on Israel by Babylon. He admitted Israel's sin but asked why an unrighteous nation like Babylon was so worthy to conquer. There is no lengthy answer in this short book. God's response is only that the righteous will live by faith. That is, he or she will trust that all accounts are eventually settled. Once again the people were instructed to live righteously.

**253. Zephaniah** was a contemporary of Jeremiah. Zephaniah's prophecy came in the years immediately preceding the fall of Jerusalem. He talked of the coming day of the Lord, which for Jerusalem was right around the corner. Yet he, too, spoke of the glorious long-term future God had in mind for his people—that a remnant of God's people would survive the day of judgment.

**254. Haggai** and the next two prophets did their work after the remnant of Israelites returned from exile in Babylon. Haggai is specifically mentioned in the Book of Ezra as being among the returning exiles. Haggai's style is compact, forceful, and at times stern. Yet he encouraged the leaders and the people not to grieve over the brokenness of the nation they were rebuilding.

**255. Zechariah** was a coworker with Haggai. He, too, is mentioned in the Book of Ezra. His writing is considerably longer and more complex than Haggai's. This book can be divided into four sections (the first three are dated, but the last is not). He described visions, some of which are as complex as those found in Ezekiel and Daniel.

**256. Malachi.** The twelfth and last of the minor prophets is more proselike than poetic, with a definite plan of argument. Malachi was concerned with the morality of the priesthood in his time. You would think that with all the warning the prophets had given before the fall of Jerusalem and all the chastening Israel had experienced that the priests would be diligent about keeping up their duties. But they weren't. Malachi warned the priests who thought they would get a "free ride" that they were in for a rude awakening.

# 11

# In the Beginning

**257. God began it all.** "In the beginning God . . ." is how the first verse of the first chapter of the first book of the Bible begins. The beginning of the history of the world is chronicled with those words!

**258. Elohim,** which originates from the Hebrew word *el,* is translated as "god." The Hebrew word *el* actually is used for reference to all general gods. Another title of God, *el elyon,* is also a derivation of this and means "the most high God" (Gen. 14:18).

**259. Yahweh** is the only name for God that is personal in nature. A Hebrew word, it is commonly translated into English versions as "Jehovah," or "the LORD" (Exod. 6:3).

**260. When creation began.** Relying on biblical sources such as the chronologies and genealogies in Genesis, numerous people have attempted to pinpoint a time and date for the precise moment of creation. Ancient Hebrew scholars placed the moment as 3761 B.C. Perhaps the most famous creation date was the one produced by Irish bishop James Ussher (1581–1656). Using Genesis, Ussher dated the moment of creation to the early morning of the twenty-third of October in 4004 B.C. (Ussher actually used the Julian calendar year of 710). Ussher's calculation was widely accepted by European Christians for centuries and was included in the margins of many editions of the King James Bible, giving it nearly divine "authority."

**261. Eden,** which means "a place of delight," is believed by some scholars to have been located at the eastern end of the Fertile Crescent, near where the Tigris and Euphrates Rivers meet the Persian Gulf.

**262. The name "Adam"** is a pun on the similar Hebrew words for "soil" and for "man." The word *Adam* is derived from the Hebrew word for "man" in the collective sense, as in humanity or humankind. It is also related to the Hebrew word *adamah,* which means "ground" or "earth." The author of Genesis used a wordplay. *Adam,* man, came from *adamah,* the ground.

**263. Not an apple.** Though legend has it that the forbidden fruit of the tree of knowledge that Eve was tempted by the serpent to taste was an apple, nowhere does the Bible identify it as one. In fact most scholars agree that the one fruit it definitely could not have been was the apple. Apples were not likely to have grown in the Bible lands in Old Testament times. However, apples were cultivated by the Egyptians, and the Romans at the time of Christ had more than twenty varieties.

**264. The legend that the apple** was the fruit on the tree of knowledge arose in the Middle Ages when artists painted pictures of Eve tasting the apple. Another source of confusion was the medieval custom of calling many different kinds of fruits "apples." Lemons were known as "Persian apples," dates as "finger apples," and pomegranates as "apples of Carthage."

**265. Apples or apricots?** The fruit meant by the Hebrew word commonly translated as "apple" was probably the apricot, which flourishes all over the Bible lands. A clue comes from Solomon, who used the same word to describe a tree: "I delight to sit in his shade, and his fruit is sweet to my taste" (Song of Sol. 2:3). Solomon seems to be describing the apricot, for even today nomads pitch their tents under its branches for shade, and it is the fruit with the sweetest taste in the Holy Land.

**266. "Apples of gold in settings of silver."** Proverbs appears to describe the apricot in this way (25:11). Not only is this a lovely poetic description of an apricot tree, it is also remarkably accurate. Its fruit is golden and the pale undersides of the leaves look silver when they turn in the breeze.

**267. Adam and Eve.** The story of creation is one of continuing wonder to believers and nonbelievers alike. Humankind *had* to come from somewhere, and the story told in Genesis 1 and 2 reveals how a creative, organized God spoke the world into existence.

**268. The fall of man.** Though Adam and Eve lived in a perfect world, they chose to disobey God and eat the forbidden fruit. Scripture is clear that such a choice led to our current situation— humankind is sinful and separated from God yet still desires peace with him.

**269. The fig tree** is the second tree named in the Bible. After eating the forbidden apricot, Adam and Eve "sewed fig leaves together and made coverings for themselves" (Gen. 3:7). The large, tough leaves of the fig tree would certainly have made adequate clothing. Fig leaves are still sewn together in the Near East to make baskets, dishes, and even umbrellas.

**270. Adam and Eve were banished from Eden** into what the Bible describes as a land of thorns and thistles. Thorns and spines grow on many different kinds of plants, but they are especially common on plants of the desert and semiarid regions of the world. Many kinds of thistles grow abundantly in the Bible lands.

**271. Adam and Eve's firstborn son,** Cain, is remembered as the first murderer for killing his brother, Abel. When God sentenced Cain to wander the earth, Cain begged for mercy and, in fear, thought that someone would kill him. So God marked him. Widely viewed as a sign of guilt, the so-called "mark of Cain" is actually a symbol of divine mercy. Opponents of the death penalty point to this first murder and God's merciful sentence on the murderer as a biblical rejection of capital punishment. For his crime Cain received a life sentence of hard labor.

**272. Who were the Nephilim?** Squeezed between the generation after Adam and the time of Noah is a curious story (Gen. 6:1–4) about the mysterious "Nephilim," briefly described as the offspring of the "sons of God." Echoing tales of Greek gods who mated with mortal women, the biblical passage calls the offspring of the angelic-human marriages "heroes of old, men of renown." They are only mentioned once more in Hebrew Scriptures, where Nephilim literally translates as "the fallen ones." Many believe they were giants possessing superhuman powers.

**273. Some early theologians thought the Nephilim** were fallen angels who were responsible for sin in the world. Whoever these "sons of God" and their children were, God was not happy with the situation. He limited human life spans to 120 years. People became so wicked that God was sorry he had made humankind on the earth, and it grieved him. "So the Lord said, 'I will wipe mankind, whom I have created, from the face of the earth—men and animals, and creatures that move along the ground and birds of the air—for I am grieved that I have made them.' But Noah found favor in the eyes of the LORD" (Gen. 6:5–8).

**274. Noah and the ark.** Genesis chapters 6 through 9 tell the story of people becoming thoroughly evil and God's judgment against them by sending forty days and nights of continual rainfall. At the same time, he worked through one faithful man, Noah, to build an ark and preserve a faithful remnant so that humankind could continue. The story of judgment and mercy resonates through the ages.

**275. Famous Renaissance artist and inventor Leonardo da Vinci** (1452–1519) was surprised to discover the fossilized remains of sea creatures while walking in the Alps, and he asked how they got there. The conventional wisdom of his day simply said it was proof that a flood once covered the earth.

**276. Almost every ancient culture** has some sort of flood or deluge myth that shares much in common with the biblical flood. In most of them the gods send a catastrophic flood to destroy the world, but one good man is told of the coming disaster and his family is saved to continue human existence. The one most like Noah's story comes from the Babylonian Gilgamesh epic. In this story, the hero, Utnapishtim, also survives the flood by building a boat, which comes to rest on Mount Nisir, which is in the same region as Noah's "mountains of Ararat."

**277. Noah** made his ark of "gopher wood" (Gen. 6:14), which probably meant the cypress tree. This wood is extremely durable. The doors of Saint Peter's in Rome are made from it and after twelve hundred years they still show no signs of decay.

**278. The Bible** does not list all of the animals that took refuge on the ark. However, those animals that survived the flood must have been the ones that were best known to the Hebrews and also those mentioned most often in the Bible through symbolism or otherwise.

**279. The first bird** Noah released was a raven, a powerful flier able to slice through the air or soar with the ease of a hawk on wings that span up to four feet. Its habitat is the mountain wilderness, and so it was just the bird to scout out any crags that might have emerged from the flooded earth. The raven is noted for its remarkable memory, so this scout would not forget the location of the ark.

**280. When the raven** failed to give Noah any sign of land, Noah sent out a dove. ("Doves" and "pigeons," by the way, refer to the same birds.) The rock dove was one of the earliest of all animals to be domesticated. There are Egyptian records, dating back five thousand years, of people rearing them in captivity for food and probably also as carrier pigeons.

**281. Very fast fliers,** the strong wings of doves make them capable of powerful flight in a straight line, despite storms and high winds. After at least five thousand years of using doves and pigeons to carry messages, we are still not certain how a pigeon "homes"—finds its way back to its roost—as the biblical dove found its way back to the ark.

**282. The second time Noah sent out the dove,** it returned before evening with an olive leaf. This was evidence that the waters had subsided enough to expose the valleys where olive trees grow.

The olive was the most important tree cultivated in the Holy Land. It is native only to the lands bordering the Mediterranean Sea.

**283. The story of Noah and the ark** yields some interesting analysis as a type of Christ. The ark itself is a type of Christ! God gave Noah every detail of how it was to be built, from its dimensions to its purpose in protecting Noah and his family from the judgment that awaited the rest of the world. Likewise, God planned every minute detail of how Jesus would redeem God's people; not a single detail was left to man. As the big boat brought earthly salvation for Noah, so Christ brings eternal salvation for all who believe in him. As the ark had but one door, so Christ is the door to God—he is the only way we can gain forgiveness for our sins and come to the Father.

**284. The families of Noah's sons** "had one language and a common speech" (Gen. 11:1). Babel was the original name for Babylon, which in Hebrew means "gate of God." Situated on the southern part of the flood plain between the Tigris and Euphrates rivers, Babylon was the site where builders attempted to erect a tower "that reaches to the heavens" (Gen. 11:4). The builders never completed the tower because their language became confused and they could no longer understand one another.

**285. With the destruction of the tower of Babel,** the Bible's story of the early history of humankind ends. Abraham, the great patriarch of the Hebrews, is a descendant of Noah's son Shem. Abraham was the man to whom God promised, "I will make you into a great nation and I will bless you; I will make your name great" (Gen. 12:2).

# 12

# Early Israel

**286. Abram** is the earliest biblical character who can be connected, rather remotely and speculatively, to recorded world history. There is still no specific proof of this individual outside of the Bible, but these are the first clues that the biblical world he lived in was the world as history knows it.

**287. In the biblical list of Abraham's ancestors** (Gen. 11:10–26), many family names are the same as those of several towns around Haran. Abraham's relatives either took their names from the towns where they lived or were important enough to give their names to these towns. Abraham's father, Terah, who is said to have worshiped idols for several years (Josh. 24:2), moved his family from Ur to Haran. Terah lived there until he died at the age of 205.

**288.** *Habiru* **(or "Hebrew")** was a word of disparagement, probably meaning "the dusty ones." It did not refer to the Hebrew people in particular but rather to all the land-hungry Semites who led a nomadic life. In the Book of Genesis (14:13), Abraham is called "the Hebrew," and so this general name was finally limited to his descendants.

**289. Abraham's journey southward** from Haran led through the entire length of Canaan, through the Negeb Desert to Egypt, and finally northward again to the Promised Land. His caravans were not like the camel caravans seen today in the deserts of the Near East. It is possible that until he reached Egypt he traveled on foot, with no beasts of burden except perhaps a few donkeys.

**290. Abram was given his new name, Abraham,** when God came to him in his ninety-ninth year. At that time he had one son. The new name meant "father of many nations." Abraham must have been puzzled over how God would bring him into a full understanding of his new name with but one child when he was already quite old.

**291. After Lot** chose to travel to the lower Jordan Valley, he settled near the wicked cities of Sodom and Gomorrah. These cities were destroyed by what the Bible calls "brimstone and fire" (Gen. 19:24 KJV). No one knows for sure when the last volcanic eruption took place in the Holy Land, but it may have been as recently as the Middle Ages. Geologists can see clear evidence that the Jordan Valley has been a center of volcanism in the past.

**292. The remains of the Twin Cities of Sin** have never been found. Myth has it that they lie buried beneath the Dead Sea. This theory may provide an explanation of why the Dead Sea area is rich in bitumen, or tar, supposedly left after the destructive "fire and brimstone." Bitumen was used in the Egyptian mummification process. Bitumen was also used for "tarring" houses and was one of the key trade items in this area.

**293. The Sodom and Gomorrah story** has always been useful as a moral tale of God destroying evil. But a subtext to the story has been even more influential. It is all about the sin to which the name Sodom is attached. This story has always been cited as one of the basic biblical injunctions against homosexuality.

**294. Abraham was given a covenant child** as was promised to him by the three angels who visited and prophesied of the event.

Sarah delivered a healthy infant son and they called him Isaac. He was a miracle—his mother was in her nineties and his father was one hundred!

**295. Hagar** was the servant of Sarah, Abraham's wife. She had become pregnant by Abraham and bore Ishmael. Sarah was jealous and treated her poorly and eventually Hagar was sent into the wilderness of Beer-sheba when Isaac was born. But God protected Hagar and her son and raised them up to be their own people. They were under Abraham's covenant, but Ishmael was not the promised son who would continue the lineage of the Hebrews.

**296. The sacrifice of Isaac.** God called Abraham to follow him to a far land and promised to make his family a great nation. Yet when Abraham finally had a son in his old age, the Lord asked him to sacrifice the boy on Mount Moriah. Instead of a pagan practice, it was a test of faith—God intervened to stop the sacrifice and provided a ram to sacrifice in the boy's place. Then, praising Abraham's faith, God promised to bless all nations through his offspring.

**297. The story of Abraham's unshakable faith** while offering Isaac is a central moment in the Bible. To many people it seems an unnecessarily cruel test of faith. Abraham doesn't even make the arguments for his own son that he made for the citizens of Sodom. His wife, Sarah, is silent in this episode, and Isaac's thoughts are not available to us either.

**298. When God stays Abraham's hand.** The passage says that Abraham "fears" God. The "fear of God" is a commonly used expression today. The Hebrew verb for "fear" can be understood two ways. Occasionally it meant being afraid, but very often the biblical "fear" meant awe or reverence for someone of exalted position. Abraham was not necessarily "afraid" of God as much as he held God in profound respect.

**299. The Bible notes that Abraham** was "very rich in cattle" (Gen. 13:2 KJV), and he is often described as having flocks and herds. In the early books of the Bible, however, the word *cattle* is believed to usually refer to sheep and goats rather than to cows.

**300. Throughout the history of the Hebrews,** even after they became a mighty nation under kings as in the glittering court of

Solomon, the simple life of the shepherd was remembered and upheld as the most desirable existence.

**301. After Sarah died at age 127,** Abraham buried her in a cave in Hebron. He purchased the burial land from the local people, the Hittites, and the verses elaborately explain the great measures Abraham took to stake a legal claim to this land. This passage is one of the oldest recorded real estate deals, a legal confirmation of possession of land that had already been divinely promised.

**302. After Sarah died, Abraham decided to marry again** and took another wife, Keturah. She birthed six more of Abraham's children. These were the ancestors of other Arabic tribes including the Midianites, who play a role in the story of Moses. When Abraham died at age 175, he was buried alongside Sarah in the cave on the site he had purchased at Hebron.

**303. Isaac's name meant "laughter."** He was the second patriarch. Isaac married Rebekah and they had two sons, Jacob and Esau, who were twins. They were never close brothers and had few similar interests. Esau was the older of the two and was a hunter. Jacob was closer to his mother and appeared crafty and the smarter of the two.

**304. The classic story of how Jacob gained the birthright,** the right to all the blessings of the firstborn son, is a story of true deceit, yet it was prophetic that Jacob gained the upper hand. God had said the "older will serve the younger." Both were ultimately blessed by God, but Jacob did use trickery to con his aged father into giving him the blessing by pretending to be Esau after getting Esau to sell his birthright for a bowl of stew.

**305. Wrestling with God.** The life of Jacob contains a number of interesting stories that make him appear more a scoundrel than a patriarch. He cheated his brother Esau and tricked his father. However, one of the strangest stories occurs in Genesis 32. While preparing to meet Esau, Jacob met God (appearing as a man) and wrestled with him all night. After having his hip torn from his socket, Jacob told the man that he would continue wrestling until he was blessed. With that God changed Jacob's name to *Israel*, which means "wrestles with God."

**306. Jacob married** two sisters, Rachel and Leah. Through deceit on the girls' father's part, Jacob ended up being tricked on his wedding night. Jacob served Laban for seven years for Laban's younger daughter, Rachel. The morning after the wedding, Jacob found he had married Leah, Laban's older daughter, instead! Laban agreed to give him Rachel, too, in exchange for another seven years of service.

**307. Eventually the two sisters and their two maids** produced twelve sons, who would become the twelve tribes of Israel. They were Reuben, Simeon, Levi, Judah, Dan, Naphtali, Gad, Asher, Issachar, Zebulun, Joseph, and Benjamin. Throughout the story of Jacob's life, God was with him. As long as Jacob remained obedient to God, he was blessed. The history of Israel would go on (and on!) all the way through the New Testament and the birth of a Savior from these early roots.

**308. Before leaving the place of her birth,** Rachel stole her father's "household gods." These small "household gods" were idols, typical of the cults in Canaan and elsewhere in Mesopotamia. Small statues of fertility symbols, they were placed in the homes. Laban caught up to Jacob's caravan and began to search for the idols. When Laban came to search Rachel's tent, she sat on a saddlebag which held her father's gods, telling them she was menstruating and couldn't get up. This story would have been told by the Israelites with derisive mockery as Rachel sat on the idols in her time of "uncleanness."

**309. The story of Joseph's "coat of many colors"** remains a favorite of many people. Joseph was the gifted son, the one who had found favor with God. He was also his father's favorite son, much to the chagrin of most of the other brothers. Jacob made Joseph the heir, even though he was the second to the youngest! He was a bold young man and his brothers eventually sold him into slavery in Egypt.

**310. God never forgot Joseph, however.** Eventually this young man who saw visions and could interpret dreams would make himself useful to Pharaoh himself! He would become a chief minister of Egypt and would be reunited with his family in their time of need during a drought affecting the whole land.

**311. Elaborate court records** survive of many of the Pharaohs before and after the presumed time of Joseph. But none of them mentions a Semite slave becoming a high official who had helped save Egypt in a time of extraordinary famine. Periodic drought and famine were not unusual in ancient times, and several were recorded, although none exactly match the biblical scenario. So we do not know who Joseph's Pharaoh was.

**312. Joseph had two sons:** Manasseh and Ephraim. The brothers were born in Egypt and would eventually be blessed by Jacob. As had happened in Joseph's own experience, God blessed the younger, Ephraim, more than the older brother, Manasseh. God's blessing continued to fall on those who were not expecting the bulk of it.

**313. They all remained in Egypt** and lived happily there until the whole generation of Joseph and his brothers passed away. Then they were oppressed by the Egyptians and used as slaves. The Egyptians feared the great numbers of Hebrew people being born and even demanded that the midwives kill the newborn males.

**314. Moses was another miracle.** He should have been killed as many of the other male infants were, but he was saved by God for a special purpose. His mother floated him down the Nile in a basket made of reeds, and he was eventually taken into the palace by the royalty of Egypt. Moses would grow up to be a great man of God and the hero of the early Israelites.

**315. Egyptian texts confirm** that about the time Moses became angered at seeing an Egyptian overseer beating a Hebrew worker, the Hebrews were engaged in dragging stones for temples built by Pharaoh Ramses II. The Bible says Moses killed the overseer and fled into the desert wilderness of the Sinai Peninsula where he would later see the bush that "burned with fire."

**316. Moses—or *Moshe* in Hebrew—**is the central human figure in the Hebrew Bible, the great lawbringer, and for Christians, the symbolic model for Jesus. Moses was saved after a king ordered the Jewish babies killed; Jesus was saved after a king ordered Jewish babies to be killed. Moses parted the waters; Jesus walked on the waters. Moses spent forty years in the wilderness; Jesus spent forty days in the wilderness. Moses went to a mountain and gave a sermon; Jesus gave a sermon on the mount. Moses delivered the covenant; Jesus delivered the new covenant.

**317. Aaron was Moses' older brother.** He was a good speaker (Moses was not) and was sent by God to help Moses ask Pharoah to let the Israelites go. He served as the first high priest of Israel. He and Moses were the leaders of the exile from Egypt.

**318. The escape from Egypt.** Moses went before Pharaoh and demanded that his people be set free. The story of Moses—who was miraculously saved and raised as royalty, then lost his position due to immature violence, only to be called by God to greatness—is a wonderful riches-to-rags-to-riches story. The plagues, the escape, and the parting of the Red Sea make it one of the most-told stories of all time.

**319. "The Song of Miriam,"** a victory chant led by the sister of Moses after the Israelites crossed the Red Sea, is thought to be one of the oldest poetic verses in Hebrew Scriptures:

> "I will sing to the LORD,
>     for he is highly exalted.
> The horse and its rider
>     he has hurled into the sea."

> Exodus 15:21

**320. The "Aaronic benediction"** was given by God to Aaron. This extremely ancient blessing is still widely used in temples and churches today among both Jews and Christians:

> "The LORD bless you
>     and keep you;
> the LORD make his face shine upon you
>     and be gracious to you;
> the LORD turn his face toward you
>     and give you peace."

> Numbers 6:24–26

**321. God brought his people out of Egypt** and they settled in the desert. The Israelites, as they had come to be called, didn't always trust God as they should. They constantly forgot what a miracle their escape from Egypt was. As a result they suffered some difficult times and were eventually forbidden to go into the Promised Land God had for them until the entire first generation of people died off.

**322. A flakelike stuff** as fine as frost, called *manna,* appeared each morning on the surface of the ground in the desert. When the ancient Israelites first encountered this miraculous provision of food from God in the desert, they asked, "What is it?!" And the name stuck. So "manna," the word the Israelites used to call the stuff on the ground, meant "whatchamacallit."

**323. The Great Commandment.** "Hear, O Israel: The LORD our God, the LORD is one. Love the LORD your God with all your heart and with all your soul and with all your strength" (Deut. 6:4–5). This is the Shema, the most commonly spoken prayer in Judaism, also traditionally called the "Great Commandment." Many Christians know it in the form that Jesus used in Mark 12:29.

**324. From out of Canaan.** As the Israelites approached the borders of the Promised Land, Moses sent out scouts who reported giants in the land. The scouts were frightened and they returned to the camp carrying clusters of grapes and pomegranates as proof that they had at least entered the land of Canaan.

# 13

# The Israelite Adventure

**325. Freed at last, the Israelites set about making a temple in which to worship God.** The tabernacle was their first place of worship. Very explicit instructions were given for how it was to be built (Exodus 26). Inside the tabernacle, which was a giant tent, were several rooms, including the Most Holy Place and the curtain separating that section from the Holy Place. The tabernacle was 75 feet by 150 feet in diameter.

**326. The tent of the tabernacle** was covered with badger skins. These skins are mentioned several times in the Old Testament. They were highly valued and were listed along with gold, jewels, and other precious objects. Most badger pelts were extremely durable and tough, making excellent waterproofing material for the tabernacle.

**327. The ark of the covenant** was the single most important object in the history of ancient Israel, though it disappeared from the Bible without mention. It was first housed in the tabernacle. After Jerusalem was destroyed in 586 B.C. the fate of the ark was never discussed. It was a huge chest that contained the stone tablets of the Ten Commandments. Above the chest stretched the wings of two cherubim.

**328. Offerings** of all sorts were an important part of worshiping as an Israelite. Leviticus details the necessary sacrifices for the burnt offering, sin offering, grain offering, fellowship offering, guilt offering, and others.

**329. The Israelites had many hostile enemies** on all sides— Philistines, Assyrians, Babylonians, Moabites, and so on. These enemies were given over at times into the Israelites' hands, but at other times God allowed them to overrun the Israelites. Throughout their history they experienced peace and prosperity as well as hardship and exile.

**330. Out of the mouth of donkeys.** Threatened by the Israelites, the king of Moab asked a magician named Balaam to come to Moab and put a curse on the Israelites. So the Mesopotamian wizard saddled up his donkey and went to help King Balak. As Balaam was riding down the road, the donkey saw an angel of the Lord and refused to move. Unable to see the angel, Balaam struck the donkey. Finally the donkey turned around and asked the magician, "What have I done to you that you have struck me three times?" God then opened Balaam's eyes and he saw the angel blocking the road. The heavenly messenger then gave Balaam specific instructions. Instead of cursing Israel, the magician gave his blessing (Numbers 22–23).

**331. Sihon was a king of the Amorites.** He refused the Israelites access to the Promised Land (it would have taken them through his land) and even marched against God's people. God allowed the Israelites to defeat Sihon and then take his territory. Throughout history God delivered many enemies into their hands.

**332. Rahab is a famous woman of the Bible.** Though a prostitute in the city of Jericho, she understood the power of the Israelites and rightly attributed it to God. When two spies came to study the city, she protected them by hiding them in her home. They escaped through her window, promising not to harm her and her family if she would leave a scarlet cord tied in her window (Joshua 2). Later she would be taken into the Israelites' people and even marry and become part of the lineage of Jesus Christ!

**333. At least six cities west of the Jordan** were destroyed approximately thirty-two hundred years ago, when the invasion under Joshua was taking place. Even a written record from Egypt exists dating from that time that tells of a pharaoh's dealings with "the people of Israel" in Canaan.

**334. After the crossing of the Jordan**, twelve river stones were set in a pile at Gilgal. The first Passover in the Promised Land was celebrated there and a mass circumcision was performed with flint knives because all the men born in the wilderness had not been circumcised. That is why Gilgal means "Hill of the Foreskins" (Joshua 5).

**335. Joshua became the leader of the Israelites after Moses died.** It was under his authority that the people at last crossed over into Canaan. He served God and was revered by the people, but he too failed at times and disobeyed God. He is perhaps most remembered for his part in the battle of Jericho.

**336. The battle of Jericho** is one of the most miraculous demonstrations of God's power to the Israelites as they became a new nation. The Israelites were instructed to march around Jericho one time each day for six days. The priests were to carry rams' horns at the front of the army. On the seventh day the priests were instructed to blow the trumpets. Then the people were all to shout. God promised Joshua that the walls would then collapse and the men would be able to go inside the city walls and take the city. And it happened just as the angel promised Joshua it would (Joshua 6).

**337. Some of the Israelites continued to disobey God** in spite of the intensity of his miracles. Achan was one such case. During the battle of Jericho, he took some of the prized gold and other precious items that belonged to God and kept them for himself. As a result the Israelites lost their next battle (Joshua 7). God punished his people repeatedly for disobeying his commands. He is ever the faithful Father, yet he is a righteous God who demands obedience.

**338. Once the Israelites were established in Canaan,** they were governed by judges, people who had usually been warriors first. God gave his people strong leaders to follow, but they didn't always do so. The Book of Judges tells of the difficulties they suffered when they did not obey God.

**339. After Joshua died, it wasn't long** before the Israelites "did what was evil in the sight of the Lord." The Israelites were soon mesmerized by the Canaanite gods: Baal, Astarte, and Asherah. It is believed that the Torah laws relating to lewd and perverse sexual practices were in response to Canaanite sexual practices.

**340. Othniel** was the first judge. When the Israelites began worshiping these Canaanite gods, God allowed Cushan-Rishathaim, a Syrian king, to overcome them. They were ruled over by the Syrians for eight years. As soon as Israel repented of their sins, God led Othniel to raise up an army to defend Israel. They defeated the Syrians handily. Othniel ruled Israel for forty years after that (Judg. 3:9–11).

**341. Ehud** is perhaps the most famous left-handed warrior in history. The Israelites had been ruled by the Moabites for some time. When Ehud, a Benjamite judge, went to pay taxes to King Eglon, he hid a sword under his cloak. Since Ehud was left-handed, and few if any people (evidently) drew swords with that hand, the king didn't suspect anything when Ehud drew his sword. He swiftly killed the king and then defeated the other Moabites. Then he continued to rule as a judge, and the Israelites lived in peace for many years (Judg. 3:15–30).

**342. Shamgar** was made judge after Ehud died. By then Israel had turned again from God and was under the power of the Canaanites and the Philistines. It was a difficult time in the history of Israel. The people were under Jabin's rule, and he was a harsh Canaanite king. Shamgar fought back and killed six hundred Philistines with a single metal-tipped stick called an oxgoad (Judg. 3:31). He could not stop Jabin, however.

**343. The two most famous military heroines** mentioned in the Old Testament are Deborah and Jael, and they both had a hand in the same victory. God spoke through Deborah to tell the general, Barak, how to defeat the Canaanites, including their king, Jabin.

Barak agreed to attack, but wanted Deborah to go with him into the battle. She did and the enemies were defeated.

**344. Sisera** was a king of Canaan. He fought hard against Israel, but his nine hundred iron chariots were no match for the rain God sent. As a result the chariots were stuck in the mud and God gave Sisera and his people over to the Israelites.

**345. Jael** became a hero of the Israelites, though she herself was a Kenite. Hers was a peaceful tribe that lived comfortably near the Israelites, thanks to her ties to Moses' father-in-law, Jethro. Jael would eventually kill Sisera when he sought refuge with her family. She lulled him to sleep in a tent and then hammered a peg through his head (Judges 4).

**346. Barak and Deborah** ruled over Israel in peace for forty years. Deborah is also famous for her victory song, a portion of which is here:

> "When the princes in Israel take the lead,
>     when the people willingly offer themselves—
>     praise the LORD! . . .
> So may all your enemies perish, O LORD!
>     But may they who love you be like the sun
>     when it rises in its strength."
>
>                                    Judges 5:2, 31

**347. Gideon is one of the most famous judges.** His victory over the Midianites was a testimony to his faith in God and his obedience to what God had ordered him to do. God told Gideon to send away all of the men who were planning to fight except for three hundred in order to show that God would take care of the people. Gideon obeyed, and God delivered the Midianites into the Israelites' hands. Later young Gideon became a judge. He was faithful to God almost to the very end. He was blessed with seventy sons (Judges 6–8).

**348. Hardly the image of a judge,** and the illegitimate son of a prostitute, Jephthah was an outcast from his father's family and became an outlaw, an ancient Hebrew "Robin Hood." He is known as the one who, after asking for God's help, made a terrible vow: He promised to sacrifice whoever greeted him if he was victorious. After he won the battle against the Ammonites, he was greeted by his own daughter, who was then sacrificed (Judges 10–11).

**349. The Philistines,** the so-called "Sea Peoples" of the Mediterranean, eventually settled on the southern coast of Canaan, in what is now the area around Gaza. From this coastal base, the Philistines pressed inland and collided with the Israelite tribes who were spreading themselves down from the hill country toward the coast. The well-organized military force of the Philistines and their considerable use of iron were a major threat to the Israelites.

**350. Samson is perhaps the most famous judge of all time.** He was not the most faithful of all judges; he was proud and did not heed God's word. He was lured into trusting Delilah, a woman paid by the Philistines to find out the secret of his immense strength. Samson would routinely kill large numbers of Philistines, thereby protecting the Israelites. Delilah easily charmed the secret out of him, using her wiles, and Samson's hair was cut. He was taken captive, blinded, and forced to stay in chains in a Philistine dungeon (Judges 13–16).

**351. Yet God heard Samson's final request:** Samson prayed for one last chance to serve God and punish the Philistines. God granted his wish with a miracle of amazing proportions. Samson was led into the Philistine temple to be mocked by many Philistines one night. The Philistines put him between two pillars of the temple. Samson pushed with the strength that God had granted him. The temple toppled over and killed the Philistines as well as himself (Judg. 16:23–30).

**352. Also living during the time of the Judges were Ruth and Boaz.** Ruth was a Moabite, but she moved to Bethlehem to be with her mother-in-law after they both lost their husbands. Ruth was accepted and married Boaz, a good and faithful man, and they were blessed with children and a happy life. Their story is yet another demonstration of how God works to bring people into his plan and to further their joy. Ruth and Boaz were the great-grandparents of King David.

**353. Samuel** was the last judge of Israel and also served as a prophet. He was born to childless parents after his mother, Hannah, promised to dedicate a child to God to serve him in the temple. God heard her prayer. Samuel was a mighty figure of Israel and helped put the first kings of the nation on the throne.

**354. Saul was the first king of Israel.** He was anointed by the prophet Samuel. He was known to be very tall and majestic of frame. God blessed Saul as long as he was obedient to God and listened to Samuel. But Saul fell away from God and suffered an unhappy ending. He became proud and jealous of David, a young man who was loyal to him and served him in battle and also on a personal level. God did not allow Saul's sins to go unpunished. During a battle, Saul and many of his family were lost; Saul killed himself in order to avoid being captured.

**355. On witches.** God told Moses, "Do not allow a sorceress (female witch) to live." King Saul visited a medium at Endor, disregarding the forbidden practice. She summoned up the spirit of the dead Samuel, who had bad news for Saul: He and his sons and the Israelites would fall to the Philistines in battle. The predictions came true as Jonathan and two of Saul's other sons were killed. Saul fell on his sword with the help of his armor-bearer.

**356. David, the youngest son of Jesse,** was anointed by Samuel to be the second king of Israel when he was only a shepherd boy. He was a faithful witness to God's amazing love and found much joy and happiness as both a warrior and a king. Yet he, too, sinned and was punished. But he came back to God and was forgiven. David was also a famous poet—many of the Psalms were written by him.

**357. David's defeat of Goliath** was his first step toward the throne and away from the fields of sheep he normally watched over. The battle pitted the underdog (a shepherd boy named David) against a mighty warrior (the Philistine Goliath). Though trained soldiers were afraid to fight the giant, David's simple faith made him courageously step forward and kill the giant using a stone thrown from a sling. The stone hit Goliath in the forehead, knocking him down. David then cut the giant's head off with his own sword. The Philistine armies fled, and David's career as a leader of Israel was born (1 Samuel 17).

# 14

# Poetry of Kings

**358. Job** is never identified as a Jew, and he wasn't a king, but his book fits with the poetic books of both King David and King Solomon. Job is thought to have lived in the Arabian Desert, somewhere between Babylon and the Holy Land. Interestingly, he was the great naturalist of the Old Testament, and he displayed a deep knowledge and an observant eye for the world around him. "Speak to the earth and it shall teach thee," he advises (Job 12:8 KJV). He followed his own advice because he describes precisely the habits of mammals, the way of birds, the patterns in the skies, the rains and the floods. He speaks knowingly of the various trees that grow along the streams, from the papyrus in the marshes to the thorny shrubs of the desert.

**359. A keen watcher of the skies.** In chapter 9 Job refers to "Arcturus, Orion, and Pleiades, and the chambers of the south" (KJV). He was aware that the stars are not scattered at random in the night sky but are fixed in unchanging patterns, one of which is the Zodiac. The Zodiac is an imaginary belt across the sky consisting of twelve groups of stars—constellations, or "chambers," as Job called them—through which the sun and moon seem to pass. Each constellation appeared to the ancients to represent the figure of some animal or a mythical being usually associated with animals.

**360. "Oh that I had wings like a dove!** for then would I fly away, and be at rest" (KJV). David, weighed down by his duties, must have wished he could take flight from his tasks. He might have selected almost any bird to express this wish in Psalm 55, yet he chose the dove for a particular reason. The former shepherd knew that while most birds can fly, only doves can take off with a sudden burst of speed and sustain their powerful flight for a long distance.

**361. David was more than a great warrior.** He was a musician who played the eight-stringed harplike instrument known as the lyre. He was also a great poet who composed about half of the Psalms. David used many descriptions of animals, birds, and plant life in the Psalms to portray poetic images.

**362. Was he a lover or a fighter?** David's eye for beauty included a passion for women as well as nature. As was the custom, many of David's wives and concubines were the result of political maneuvers that expanded and secured David's kingdom territory.

**363. The habits of the Palestinian house sparrow** were so well known that Psalm 102 uses it as a symbol of desolation: "I watch, and am as a sparrow alone upon the house top" (KJV). Here is an intentional contradiction, for it is difficult to visualize a lone sparrow. House sparrows are highly gregarious birds; they seek food in large flocks and at night they group in protected places, such as under the roof eaves of buildings. This psalm's unlikely picture of a single sparrow evokes a feeling of utter loneliness and abandonment.

**364. "I am like a pelican of the wilderness"** (KJV). Also found in Psalm 102, this too is David's lament. The white pelican is abundant around the inland lakes and rivers of Africa and Eurasia where it preys on fish, but many Bible readers have wondered what the pelican was doing in the wilderness. In the Bible the word *wilderness* refers to any unpopulated place, such as a mountain, desert, or marsh. Pelicans are often found living in the deserts of the Bible lands, so long as there is an inland lake within flying distance.

**365. The shortest psalm (117)** has just two verses and the longest psalm is just two psalms later (119). It is also the longest chapter in the Bible, and longer than some whole Bible books—such as Obadiah, Philemon, and Jude.

**366. It appears that this collection** was begun as something of a hymnbook for temple worship in Jerusalem. Words such as *selah*, *maskil*, and *miktam* are found throughout the book to give direction to those who would speak or chant these psalms in public worship.

**367. The Book of Psalms** is really five different books of songs and poems; all connect our relationship to God. Book 1 includes Psalms 1–41; book 2 is Psalms 42–72; book 3 includes Psalms 73–89; book 4 has Psalms 90–106; and book 5 has Psalms 107–150.

**368. Acrostic poems** are found throughout Jewish literature. Psalm 119, the longest chapter in the Bible, is an acrostic poem—every new stanza begins with the successive letter of the Hebrew alphabet. Psalm 112 is similar, with each line beginning with the next letter of the alphabet. This was not only poetic, but also aided in the memorization of the psalm.

**369. The Penitential Psalms** is the title given to seven psalms that express deep repentance over sin: Psalm 7, 32, 38, 51, 102, 130, and 143. All but two are attributed to King David—most notably Psalm 51, which is his lament over committing adultery with Bathsheba.

**370. The Messianic Psalms** are Old Testament psalms that relate information about the coming Messiah. They were generally quoted by the Lord Jesus or the New Testament writers in reference to him. These include Psalm 22, 40, 41, 45, 69, 72, and 118.

**371. The Psalms of Ascent** are the songs that were sung by Jewish pilgrims as they traveled upward from the surrounding areas of Palestine to the city of Jerusalem for festivals. The songs tell of looking up to the hills, seeing the walls of Jerusalem, and observing the many people gathering together to worship. They end with a joyous shout of praise as the pilgrims finally arrive at the gates of the temple.

**372. The Philistines** held a monopoly on the manufacture of iron, and in this way they exerted control over the Israelites. The Philistines jealously guarded the secrets of the complicated smelting process, and they prevented the Israelites from stocking up on iron swords and shields by not allowing them to have smiths in their territory. Only after the first two kings of Israel, Saul and David, defeated the Philistines did the metal come into common use. The Israelites then learned the techniques of iron-making. Even the Hebrew words for "knife" and "helmet" came from the Philistines.

**373. The conquest of the city of Jebus** was one of David's victories. He changed the name to Jerusalem, which means "City of Peace." Jerusalem is situated on a limestone ridge about twenty-five hundred feet above sea level. To the south and west is the valley of Hinnom (or Gehenna), which was used to burn refuse. By New Testament times Gehenna had become a symbol for hell, probably because of the fires constantly burning there.

**374. Solomon became king** in the year 961 B.C. and reigned for thirty-nine years. The name *Solomon* is derived from the Hebrew word for "peace," and Solomon indeed lived up to his name. Under his reign Jerusalem became one of the most important cities in the Near East.

**375. Solomon** was the wisest man who ever lived; he was "wiser than all men" (1 Kings 4:31 KJV). God had asked him what he wanted more than anything, and Solomon asked for wisdom in order to better rule the people of Israel. His wisdom was unsurpassed, and the people lived very well under his rule. A beautiful temple was even built, but sadly many of the Israelites, including Solomon, eventually began sacrificing to other gods. God raised up armies to fight against him and his people, but he made a decision not to take the nation from Solomon's rule . . . he would spare Solomon that for his father's sake. Instead Israel would be lost during the reign of Solomon's son, Rehoboam.

**376. Knowing it all.** Not only did Solomon speak over three thousand proverbs and write more than a thousand songs, some of which come down to us in the books of Proverbs and the Song of Solomon, he could also speak knowingly on any subject. And he was obviously an authority on natural history. The Bible says that he could lecture on "trees, from the cedar tree that is in Lebanon even unto the hyssop that springeth out of the wall: he spake also of beasts, and of fowl, and of creeping things, and of fishes" (1 Kings 4:33 KJV).

**377. The cedar** was the largest tree that Solomon could have known, and the little fragrant herb, the hyssop, was among the smallest. Unlike modern hyssop, the plant Solomon spoke of is believed to have been one of the marjorams, members of the mint family that grow clusters of white flowers among rocks and in crevices in walls. Under these conditions it is among the smallest flowering plants in the Holy Land.

**378. The cedar of Lebanon** was the largest and most noble tree growing in the Bible lands. It was once abundant in the regions of Lebanon, Syria, and Turkey. It towered as high as 120 feet, and the diameter of its trunk sometimes reached eight feet. It had a fragrant gum that made walking in a cedar grove a delight. Its wood not only was a beautiful reddish color, but it also resisted decay and attack by insects.

**379. A gardener on a grand scale.** The Bible describes Solomon as a gardener (Eccl. 2:4–6). No one has yet found the exact location of Solomon's gardens, but they must have been quite close to the palace. A few miles outside of Jerusalem are three large reservoirs that have traditionally been called the Pools of Solomon, and they may be the reservoirs he built to provide water for his gardens.

**380. The most unusual of Solomon's gardens** must have been the one devoted to spices, for Solomon's far-flung trade with Arabia and India brought him many exotic plants. One of the prizes of the spice garden was spikenard, which was found in the Himalaya Mountains of Asia. The dried stems became an important trade item in the ancient world.

**381. Dried spikenard** was transported across Asia by camels and stored in alabaster boxes to preserve its fragrance. That is the reason spikenard was extraordinarily expensive, as John points out when he states that Mary anointed the feet of Jesus with "a pound of ointment of spikenard" (John 12:3 KJV).

**382. Acacia,** the "shittim wood" referred to often in the Bible, has many uses. Fine-grained and durable, its wood was suitable for beautiful things like the ark of the covenant, the altar of the tabernacle, and the mummy coffins of the Egyptians. Various species of acacia also provide perfumes, gum arabic, medicine, food for cattle, and firewood.

**383. An alliance with the Phoenicians** was one of the most enterprising of Solomon's many ventures. The Bible never refers to the Phoenicians by name but instead calls them the people of Tyre, Sidon, or Gebal, the three main cities from which the Phoenicians sent out trading voyages to all parts of the ancient world. The word *Phoenicians* comes from the Greek word for "reddish-purple," which refers to the dye the Phoenicians prepared from species of murex, a marine snail. The murex has a gland that secretes a milky white fluid as a defense against predators, but when exposed to light and air, the fluid turns purple and is a permanent dye on fabric.

**384. "Tarshish ships."** This biblical reference to the ships of Solomon refers to those that were built via an agreement Solomon negotiated with his Phoenician neighbor, King Hiram of Tyre. Together they obtained skilled workmen to build him a fleet of merchant ships. No one knows exactly what the ships looked like, but they were probably a mix between the Phoenician battleships and merchant ships. Solomon's fleet was based near his smelters, at Eziongeber on the Gulf of Aqaba. From there his ships sailed with metal and other items to a place known as Ophir.

**385. After Solomon's death** between 930 and 925 B.C., political and religious differences quickly shattered the kingdom built by David and Solomon. The ten tribes in the north broke away from the southern tribes of Judah and Benjamin, and two weaker kingdoms were left: Judah in the south and Israel in the north.

**386. The call of wisdom** is made throughout the first ten chapters of Proverbs. Solomon, who was given great wisdom from God, says in Proverbs 8:22 that wisdom was the first creation of God. It's interesting that Solomon always refers to wisdom in the feminine sense: "She calls out . . ."

**387. Canticles or the Song of Songs** is a set of love poems shared between a man and a woman. Some of the images are so mature that Jewish boys were not allowed to read it until they reached adulthood. Many people have questioned its place in Scripture, but Jewish leaders decided in ancient times that the book is allegorical—the man chasing a woman is a depiction of God pursuing sinful Israel. In medieval times Christian scholars suggested that the book also represented Christ pursuing the church.

**388. "Solomon's sword"** is the phrase used to describe a wise choice. It comes from the time two women, both claiming to be the mother of an infant, approached King Solomon and asked him to settle their dispute. Solomon asked for a sword, announcing he would cut the child in half. With that the real mother insisted that the baby not be harmed and instead be given to the other woman. The king, recognizing that the true mother would intervene for the baby's welfare, awarded the child to her.

**389. "Turn, Turn, Turn."** During the 1960s, there may have been no more widely quoted Bible verses than the words from Ecclesiastes. They provided Pete Seeger with the lyrics that eventually became a hit single for the Byrds. Americans of that era may recall that President Kennedy admired these verses so much that they were read at his funeral.

# 15

# Prophets Speak

**390. Prophets and priests** played an important role in early Israel, though many of the prophets do not have books named after them. The purpose of these godly men was to serve as messengers from God to the people. The prophets and priests received orders from God and acted upon them.

**391. Moses said God would raise up** prophets like him in the generations to follow. And God did. Generally keeping a low profile, the prophets did not possess administrative power like the kings. And they had no place in the tabernacle or temple rituals like the priests. They simply spoke the mind of God as it was given to them. Unlike the kingship and the priesthood, the position of prophet could not be passed on to one's descendants. God individually chose each one.

**392. Nathan served as a prophet in the time of David and Solomon.** It was his responsibility to confront David after David stole a soldier's wife, made her pregnant, and then had the soldier killed in order to cover up his deceitful behavior. When Nathan confronted David for his behavior, David repented, but God took the child born of the woman, Bathsheba, as a punishment. However, the next child David and Bathsheba conceived was Solomon, who would be king.

**393. Elijah trusted God completely,** so much so that when King Ahab appointed prophets to worship the false god Baal, Elijah told him no more rain would fall. Three years after the drought began, when Israel was literally starving, Elijah had a contest with the Baal prophets to see which deity would answer their prayers—God or the false god Baal. The people were brought to their senses by the sign of a soaked altar bursting into flame, and they came back to God.

**394. As one of only two men who never died,** Elijah was truly a special prophet of God. Enoch, a man who walked with God, was the other. Elijah was taken up to heaven in a chariot of fire, but before he was taken he appointed Elisha, his servant, to succeed him.

**395. Even though Elijah and Elisha were** two of the most prominent prophets in the days of the northern kingdom, no book is named after them. Because of this we can assume that the seventeen books of prophecy in the Bible are just a sampling of all that the prophets spoke.

**396. The books of prophecy.** This section of the Bible is composed of seventeen books beginning with Isaiah and ending with Malachi, closing out the Old Testament. Like the books of poetry, these books don't extend the time line of Israel's history; rather, they fill in the one laid down by the books of history. Apart from Job, most of the books of poetry were associated with the kings of Israel's glory days. By contrast the books of prophecy were associated mainly with the period of Israel's decline and fall.

**397. Prophecy in the Old Testament** was not so much a telling of the future as it was an urgent statement made on behalf of God to his people. Certain elements of Hebrew prophecy spoke of the future in terms that human behavior could not change, but most of it offered God's people a choice and often stated the harsh consequences if the Israelites chose to disobey.

**398. Both the major and minor prophets** are organized in historical order. This doesn't mean the minor prophets followed the majors in history, however. They coexisted with them. Hosea, for example, was a contemporary of Isaiah. Since the fall of Jerusalem is dated by historians at 586 B.C., all the books of prophecy—major and minor—can be dated within a century or two of that date.

**399. Majors and Minors, part 1.** The distinction is made by the length of each book. Isaiah, for example, is longer than all twelve of the minor prophets put together. Although Lamentations is short, Jeremiah was a major prophet, and the full title is "The Lamentations of Jeremiah."

**400. Majors and Minors, part 2.** Israel's prophets were not the type of people to include on your invitation list to a party. The Hebrew prophets denounced evil, corruption, and immorality. The three longest prophetic books, Isaiah, Jeremiah, and Ezekiel, along with Daniel and Lamentations, have traditionally been labeled the "Major Prophets." The other twelve books are called the "Minor Prophets."

**401. Jonah was cast into the sea** by the sailors around him in order to stop the raging sea. The prophet knew God had sent the storm after he refused to go and minister to Nineveh, the capital of the Assyrian Empire. When he was thrown overboard, the sea calmed, but Jonah was swallowed by a big fish. Many believe the fish was a whale, but it is also possible that it was a shark that "saved" Jonah. He returned to Nineveh after spending three days in the belly of the big fish.

**402. The plant that God appointed to grow and shade Jonah** after he finished preaching at Nineveh is sometimes translated a "gourd plant" and sometimes simply a "plant." It is believed that the writer meant for his readers to imagine the castor bean. In hot climates it grows very fast and often seems like a tree, with huge umbrella-like leaves that make wonderful shade. The Hebrews valued the oil of its beanlike seeds and used it widely in lamps and ceremonial rites.

**403. Nineveh's demise in 612 B.C.** brought the city to its end. Nineveh fell after a two-month siege carried out by an alliance among Medes, Babylonians, and Scythians. The attackers destroyed

Nineveh by releasing the Khoser River into the city, where it dissolved the buildings' sun-dried bricks. This was a remarkable fulfillment of Nahum's prophecy: "The gates of the rivers shall be opened, and the palace shall be dissolved" (Nah. 2:6). Nineveh was lost for well over two thousand years.

**404. At the forefront.** In the period of the divided kingdom, the focus of the Bible books moves away from the kings to the ministries of a series of "prophets," those who spoke on the behalf of God after receiving divine messages through dreams or visions. Prophets tried to counsel—usually with little success—the rulers and people of Israel and Judah. The prophets became crucial biblical characters who overshadowed the kings and took their message to the entire nation.

**405. Hosea** suffered greatly as a prophet. His name means "Save, oh God!" His was a unique task: to marry a prostitute and live as a faithful husband to her. Their relationship paralleled what Israel was doing to God—God was a faithful husband to a harlot nation. Hosea thus could speak from experience and feel personally what great pain God must suffer when his people abandon him repeatedly.

**406. Gomer** was the wife Hosea was sent to marry. She bore three children to Hosea, though none of them were likely his own children. God provided names for each of the children, but they were not names to rejoice over. Rather they were fateful reminders of what Israel had become. Their names were Jezreel (in honor of a massacre that took place in Jezreel for which God was going to punish the Israelites); Lo-Ruhamah, which means "not loved"; and Lo-Ammi, which means "not my people."

**407. God's chosen people.** One of the most significant lines in Amos is the prophet's message to Israel from God: "You only have I chosen of all the families of the earth; therefore I will punish you for all your sins" (3:2). This is the essence of the Jews' designation as the "chosen people." God's covenant with the people did not entitle them to special favors; rather, being chosen increased their responsibility.

**408. Amos** was the first prophet to have his words written down. One of the more interesting facts about his book is that he used the lion to emphasize that his mission was to bring the Hebrews back to righteousness. No other wild animal is mentioned so often in the Bible as the lion. It appears in thirty-one of the sixty-six books of the Old and New Testaments.

**409. Lions were still abundant in the Bible lands** when Amos lived, and they ranged from Africa across the Near East to India. In the Holy Land itself, the lion was exterminated by about the time of the Crusades in the Middle Ages. It vanished from Egypt in the last century, and the last wild lion seen in the Near East was captured in Iran in 1923. Hunting lions was an ancient sport in the Bible lands, and many pictures show them being captured in nets and pits. Like many other Near Eastern monarchs, King Darius of Persia kept a den of lions—into which Daniel was cast.

**410. Micah** lived after Amos and Hosea. He prophesied of a future king who would be born in Bethlehem. He looked forward to that time as the current kings he suffered with consistently led the people toward idol worship and other forms of sin.

**411. Jehoiada** and his wife saved the line of kings from the wrath of King Ahaziah's mother, Athaliah, who tried to seize the throne by killing the entire family. Jehoiada was chief priest at the time. They stole Ahaziah's baby, Joash, and hid him for six years. Then they overthrew Athaliah and put Joash on the throne to reinstate his lineage.

**412. Following the reign of Manasseh,** a notorious king of Judah who reintroduced idol worship, a crucial moment in biblical history occurred in 621 B.C. During the reign of King Josiah, an ideal king who reigned for thirty-one years after taking the throne at age eight, a scroll that was about to be removed from the temple was discovered by a priest. When Josiah read the scroll, he tore his clothes in anguish because he knew how far the people had fallen from God. He began vigorous reforms and removed all pagan items from Jerusalem.

**413. Hilkiah** was the high priest who found the scroll that brought King Josiah to his knees. Together he and the young king tried to bring the people back to God.

**414. The longest prophetic book** in Hebrew Scripture, Isaiah has had a remarkable impact on our language. Perhaps more than any other book of Hebrew prophecy, Isaiah has played a central role for Christians and has even been called the "the fifth Gospel" because so many of the book's prophecies were fulfilled in the life of Jesus.

**415. The Book of Isaiah** has two distinct halves. The first thirty-nine chapters seem to have been written before the Babylonian conquest of Israel, but the rest of the book was clearly written after that event. That has led scholars to suggest there were two authors or possibly even two different prophets named Isaiah.

**416. Many well-worn phrases were born in Isaiah.** Besides providing Handel with wonderful lyrics, Isaiah has yielded phrases commonly used even today:

> "White as snow"
> "Neither shall they learn war any more"
> "The people that walked in darkness"
> "And a little child shall lead them"
> "They shall mount up with wings as eagles"
> "Be of good courage"
> "Like a lamb to the slaughter"

**417. The Servant Songs** is the name given to the passages of Scripture in Isaiah 42, 49, 50, 52, and 53 describing an innocent man who endures great pain. Many Jewish scholars did not know what to do with these passages and could not reconcile them to the images of the Messiah coming as a mighty king. But Christians from earliest times have applied them to Jesus Christ, who suffered greatly for the sins of all humankind.

**418. Christians and Jews disagree** on a key portion of Isaiah's prophecies found scattered throughout Isaiah chapters 42, 49, 50, 52, and 53 in songs that speak of a "suffering servant of God." When Isaiah speaks of a despised, rejected man of suffering who is led like a lamb to slaughter, Christians see another symbolic prophecy of Jesus. Jewish readers, on the other hand, prefer to view this as either a reference to Isaiah himself, the prophet who suffered because his words were unpopular, or to the people of Israel, who suffer for the nation's sins.

**419. Huldah, the wife of Shallum,** is one of the most noteworthy Hebrew prophetesses. She was active in ministry during the days of King Josiah. When the Book of the Law was found in the temple, the religious leaders came to her and asked what God wanted the nation to do. This "Book of the Law" is generally thought to be an early version of Deuteronomy, which places special emphasis on removing any trace of idolatry from the worship of God. For the first time since the time of the judges, before the rise of the monarchy in Israel, the Passover was properly celebrated.

**420. The prophet Jeremiah** warned of the oncoming destruction by hostile empires, and he said that sinful people would become "meat for the fowls of the heaven, and for the beasts of the earth" (Jer. 7:33 KJV). By "fowls" that would feast on the slain, Jeremiah undoubtedly meant vultures, because they feed on dead animals. The griffon is a huge vulture in the Holy Land, particularly in the mountainous areas. Although it is large and powerful, it never kills its own prey, and it will not feed on any animal that still shows signs of life. It is a remarkably clean bird in its habits, bathing almost as often as it finds water.

**421. The Babylonians came.** They laid waste to the countryside and were on the verge of capturing Jerusalem just as Jeremiah had foretold. Yet on the eve of destruction, Jeremiah did a strange thing. He bought a piece of real estate, a field near his home village. He paid seventeen shekels of silver for it, had the deed signed, sealed, and witnessed, and then instructed Baruch to put the deed in a clay jar so that it could be preserved for a long time. For just as he believed that God would surely destroy the nation of Judah, Jeremiah also believed that God would build it up again. "Is there no balm in Gilead?" Jeremiah cried out and answered his own question by refusing to despair. God would not forsake his people, no matter how faithless they had been.

**422. Jeremiah is believed** to be the author of the Book of Lamentations. In chapter three, the writer cries out:

> I am the man who has seen affliction
>      by the rod of his wrath.
> He has driven me away and made me walk
>      in darkness rather than light;

indeed he has turned his hand against me
    again and again, all day long.
He pierced my heart
    with arrows from his quiver.
I became the laughingstock of all my people;
    they mock me in song all day long.
He has filled me with bitter herbs,
    and sated me with gall.

                 verses 1–3, 13–15

**423. Origin of the term *Jews.*** In the year 587 B.C. the holy city lay in ruins, and its people were led off to captivity in Babylon after the armies of King Nebuchadnezzar overran Judah and conquered Jerusalem. Their name changed to "Jews" (from the Hebrew *Yehudi,* which means "belonging to the tribe of Judah"). They kept alive their faith and their way of life during the years of exile.

**424. Habakkuk** is thought to have been a prophet around the time of Jeremiah. He struggled with how God would want his people, despite how badly they were behaving, to come under the influence of an even more ungodly people—the Babylonians. God was faithful to his prophet and assured Habakkuk to trust him for the answer.

**425. Ezekiel** spoke knowingly about the land and its life. Scholars disputed for a long time about what animal he meant by "the great dragon" (Ezek. 29:3 KJV), until archaeologists excavated ancient Babylon and discovered the remains of an enormous gate that was ordered to be built by Nebuchadnezzar. The ruins of the Ishtar Gate showed decorations with rows of animal sculptures—at least 575 figures in all. One of the animals is a fantastic beast: the Sirrush or Dragon of Babylon.

**426. Why a dragon?** No one knows for certain why the image of the Sirrush was placed on the gates, but Nebuchadnezzar ordered these words inscribed on it: "Fierce bulls and grim dragons I put and thus supplied the gates with such overflowing rich splendor that all humanity may view it with wonderment." It is possible that the figures were intended to impress or even frighten the Medes and Persians. So although actual dragons never existed, sculptured figures of them must have been seen by Ezekiel during the exile in Babylon.

**427. The valley of dry bones** was a graveyard to which the prophet Ezekiel was commanded to preach. As he did so Ezekiel watched the bones reattach to one another and come to life—an image of the spiritually dead nation of Israel coming back to life by the power of God's Word. This event, recorded in Ezekiel 37, is one of several strange visions of the prophet.

**428. The period of the exile in Babylon,** lasting approximately from 586 to 538 B.C., deeply impacted Judaism and the Bible. Without the temple in Jerusalem as the focal point of Yahweh worship, the Jews were forced to create a new form of communal ritual with the earliest beginnings of the synagogue as their center for prayer, Torah study, and teaching.

**429. The spirit of hope to return to Jerusalem** and restore the temple gave many exiled Jews a purpose. They began to look for a Messiah, a new leader or savior. However, only a minority of the Jews took advantage of the offer to return to Judah and rebuild Jerusalem. Many of these people had lived in Babylon for two generations and intermarriage had become common.

**430. The Hebrew Bible** gained much of its present shape during the exiled years in Babylon. The Pentateuch, or Torah, approached the form it now holds, and the history of Israel, from Joshua through 1 and 2 Kings, and the earliest prophetic writings, were all most likely composed during the exile.

**431. Jeshua** was allowed to return to Jerusalem after nearly fifty years of captivity by King Cyrus of Persia. This young man, whose name means "the Lord is salvation," led the way for Jews to begin worshiping once again. He served as chief priest and helped to lead the effort to rebuild the temple.

**432. The beginnings of the diaspora,** the great dispersal of Jews throughout the Mediterranean world and eventually into Europe, is marked by the period of exile and return. While in Babylon some Jews had entered official government service, such as Nehemiah, "a cupbearer" to one Persian king, and Mordecai, who also served a Persian king in the Book of Esther.

**433. Daniel was a statesman, not a prophet.** As a result, Jewish scholars do not place this book among the prophetic books. However, because Daniel had the gift of prediction, the New Testament calls him a "prophet" (Matt. 24:15). Daniel saw many symbols in his prophetic visions, and he often recorded them without attempting to interpret what they meant.

**434. Starting in 538 B.C.,** about seventy years after the destruction of Jerusalem, Jews began returning to their holy city. The Book of Ezra describes the exiles' return. Ezra was a priest who led a group of Jews to their homeland. He was accompanied by some seventeen hundred Babylonian Jews, including some Levites. A census was recorded of who returned to the Promised Land. Much of this book deals with temple worship and its responsibilities. Ezra taught the details of the law of Moses so that Jews could reinstate the practices in the Promised Land.

**435. In Jewish history, law, and theology,** Ezra is a character of great significance. Some Hebrew scholars rank him second only to Moses as a lawgiver and prophet, and he's considered by many as the second founder (after Moses) of the Jewish nation. Not only did Ezra reinstate the law and temple worship practices, he required that all Jewish men get rid of their foreign wives and children. Ezra ends poignantly with the words, "All these had married foreign women, and some of them had children by these wives."

**436. Around 520 B.C.,** Haggai came onto the scene. The work of rebuilding the temple had nearly stopped. Haggai cheered the people on to continue the effort. He also gave great comfort to the other two priests who were hard at work. Within four years the work was done and the temple was rebuilt.

**437. The Judah of the return from Babylon** was a far cry from Solomon's empire, and the second temple, completed in 516 B.C., was modest, despite the fact that Cyrus provided funding for the rebuilding of the temple. All the gold and silver vessels that had been salvaged from the original temple and taken to Babylon were returned to Jerusalem. But never again in Scripture is the fate of Judaism's most sacred object, the ark of the covenant, mentioned.

**438. At the rededication** of the city of Jerusalem in 445 B.C., all the Jewish people and all who could hear with understanding gathered at the square in front of the Water Gate. Ezra began to read the Book of Moses before the assembly, "which was made up of men and women and all who were able to understand. And all the people listened attentively to the Book of the Law" (Neh. 8:3). This verse refers to the fact that most Jews no longer understood Hebrew. By the time of the return, Aramaic, a related Semitic language, had replaced Hebrew as the common language.

# 16

# The New Testament Writings

**439. The four Gospels** follow closely in the tradition of the books of history we saw in the Old Testament—words spoken and deeds done. Little is told of the inward thoughts and motivations of the various people in the stories. The Gospels tell how Jesus was a descendant of David, which was an essential requirement of the Messiah, according to the prophecies of Scripture.

**440. Matthew** was written by a former tax collector named Matthew. His book covers the lineage of Jesus and also tells the story of much of his ministry, including the Beatitudes.

**441. The Beatitudes** are a well-known portion of Scripture from Christ's Sermon on the Mount in which he blessed certain types of people. Matthew 5 records that Jesus blessed the poor in spirit, those who mourn, the meek, those who hunger and thirst for righteousness, the merciful, the pure in heart, the peacemakers, and those who are persecuted for righteousness' sake—all of which describe the people who would populate the kingdom of God. However the actual word *beatitude* doesn't appear in Scripture. It's from the Latin word for "blessed" and was made popular by the Vulgate.

**442. The parables** are the stories Jesus used to convey spiritual truth. They were essentially comparisons—"The kingdom of heaven is like a treasure hidden in a field" or "Everyone who hears these words and puts them into practice is like a wise man who built a house." While his concrete images made the parables memorable, they also puzzled people who could not always follow Christ's meaning.

**443. Mark** is a Gospel that details Jesus' service to those he called and preached to. Jesus' portrayal as the great servant can be found in this Gospel, which was written by someone we know very little about.

**444. Luke** opens his Gospel by saying that "many" had attempted to write an account of Jesus' life and ministry, but that he himself is doing so because God has given him "perfect understanding of all things from the very first" (Luke 1:3 KJV). God not only gave the Gospel writers firsthand exposure as eyewitnesses to the events of Jesus' ministry, but also perfect understanding. Luke is especially forthright about Christ the man.

**445. John, perhaps the most famous** book of the whole Bible in terms of its saving message, is a description of both Christ's deity and his redeeming work for sinners. The Gospel was written by the "disciple whom Jesus loved," John.

**446. John** was compelled to address the question of how a flesh-and-blood man could also be a divine being as Jesus was. The notion of gods having sex with humans was commonplace in many pagan traditions, especially among the Greeks. But to make it clear that the birth of Jesus was of God in the flesh, the Gospels described the virgin birth. Other pagan writings did not.

**447. The four Gospels therefore tell** of all aspects of Jesus: Matthew of his right to be called "King," Mark of his title as "Greatest Servant," Luke of his completely human nature, and John of his being the Savior of the world—God's only Son.

**448. The Book of Acts** was written by Luke, also the author of the Gospel of Luke. He begins with a salutation to Theophilus and makes reference to the "first account I composed" (the Gospel of Luke). Luke's two books could be titled, "The Acts of Jesus" and "The Acts of the Apostles." They comprise a two-volume history of New Testament times. The events in Acts take place over several decades. As the books of Moses established the historical framework for the Old Testament, so the Gospels and Acts establish the framework for the New Testament.

**449. The apostles' letters** are sometimes called epistles. The word *epistle* helps convey that there was a formal or public element to these letters. These last twenty-two books of the Bible were personal letters in that they often specify the names of both the sender and the recipient(s). The fact that no point is made of the authors' identities implies how unimportant the issue is. The apostles were charged with the responsibility of spreading Jesus' message faithfully, and that in and of itself gave the writings authority in the eyes of Christ's followers.

**450. Romans.** In this letter Paul writes to the disciples in Rome. Normally he wrote to communities of disciples that he himself had established. Romans is an exception, for in this case he wrote in advance of his first visit. Misunderstandings about the message of Jesus were complex, so Paul gives an extended explanation of his understanding of the message. He also deals with the complexities of Jewish versus Gentile perspectives.

**451. First Corinthians.** Corinth was a city in southern Greece. Acts 18 describes how Paul spent eighteen months there. This letter is written some time after that. Parts of this letter are difficult to follow because Paul goes straight into his answers to the Corinthians' problems without restating what they were. First Corinthians 13, the famous love passage, is timeless and universal.

**452. Second Corinthians.** By the time this letter was written, Paul had to make a defense of his ministry. Recurring problems at Corinth and the infusion of false teachings had sullied his reputation. In this wonderfully moving letter, Paul states that the purpose of the defense is not to protect his reputation but to defend the truth for those he had taught.

**453. Galatians** begins a series of shorter letters. Galatia was a region situated on the eastern side of Asia Minor. The letter was therefore addressed more broadly than the letters to Rome and Corinth. The Epistle of Galatians was to be read by various gatherings of disciples in various cities of Galatia. The purpose of the letter was straightforward: to protest and refute false teaching that had taken root in that region.

**454. Ephesians.** Ephesus was a seaport on the western coast of Asia Minor. In New Testament times this region was called Asia. This letter was very general in nature and served as an explanation of God's design, followed by specific instructions for everyday living. It was intended for communities beyond Ephesus as well.

**455. Philippians.** This letter is as specific as Ephesians is broad. Philippi was a city in northern Greece. Paul preached there on his second major journey. The people in Philippi held Paul in high esteem. He was sending words of encouragement to them during a time of persecution. Ironically Paul seems to be writing from jail. Sharing his hope, he writes of his intent to return to them at some future time.

**456. Colossians.** Colosse was a city located due east of Ephesus. This letter is very similar to Ephesians, except much shorter. As the letter ends, it gives instructions to send it on to Laodicea, another nearby city.

**457. First Thessalonians.** Thessalonica was a city in northern Greece. It was just down the road from Philippi. Paul's first visit there was recorded in Acts 17. As usual he was met with two different responses: enthusiastic acceptance and severe resistance. Paul wrote this letter to strengthen and encourage the believers there. Above all he urges them to look for "the day of the Lord" when everything will be made right.

**458. Second Thessalonians.** Sometime after the disciples at Thessalonica got Paul's first letter, they began to wonder whether "the day of the Lord" might have come and gone. Paul quickly assured them that indeed it had not. He urged them to continue imitating Jesus and loving the people around them.

**459. The Pastoral Letters** are the instructions of Paul to two young Christian ministers. Detailing useful advice about church leadership, particularly the importance of setting high moral standards, the books of 1 Timothy, 2 Timothy, and Titus have a fatherly tone as Paul writes to his young protégés.

**460. First Timothy.** Timothy was Paul's best-known helper. He is first mentioned in Acts 16. Paul met him on one of his journeys, and the two later agreed to work together. Paul writes to Timothy as a father would to a son, so there was likely a significant age difference between them, as well as a bond of love. The message of this book can be summed up with the words "The goal of this command is love, which comes from a pure heart and a good conscience and a sincere faith" (1 Tim. 1:5).

**461. Second Timothy.** Paul's second letter to Timothy was written when Paul was facing imminent death. Though the Scriptures don't record it, modern historians generally agree that Paul was beheaded in Rome for continuing to preach the gospel. This letter to Timothy was apparently written in anticipation of that event and is extremely moving. Paul charges Timothy to continue the good fight of faith.

**462. Titus.** Though Titus comes after 2 Timothy in the Bible, it was obviously written sometime before it because it contains none of Paul's immediate anticipation of death. Titus was another helper and coworker of Paul's. This letter is structured much like 1 Timothy. Paul reminds Titus to give attention to instruction and to the appointment of others who could help spread the message.

**463. Philemon** barely takes up a page in most Bibles. Though the title is "Philemon," it is also addressed to Apphia, Archippus, and the group of disciples that met in their house. The subject of the letter was a runaway slave of Philemon's named Onesimus. Paul ran across Onesimus and urged him to return home. At the same time, Paul encouraged Philemon not only to forgive Onesimus but to treat him as a brother rather than a slave.

**464. Hebrews.** Though the King James Version of the Bible attributes this letter to Paul, most modern English versions do not. The uncertainty stems from the fact that if Paul did write this letter, he failed to specify such a fact in the text as he had in all his other letters. Regardless of who wrote this epistle, it is distinctly different from any of the other letters in the Bible.

**465. The Book of Hebrews** is the only anonymous letter in the New Testament. It is placed at the end of Paul's letters in our New Testament specifically because the collectors of the Canon were not sure if it was written by Paul or not. We're also not sure of the intended recipients, though it was widely circulated in the early church. Still, the focus of the letter is clear: Jesus is our Great High Priest, the mediator between holy God and sinful man.

**466. The Christian Hall of Fame** is the title often given to Hebrews 11, which begins with Abel and proceeds to list the key figures of the Old Testament. Since it was probably intended for Jewish Christians, the list emphasizes Abraham and Moses but goes on to include the many believers who suffered persecution and martyrdom for the cause of the faith.

**467. James.** It is believed the author of this book was James, the brother of Jesus and leader of the Jerusalem council. James was written most likely for Jewish Christians, as it is addressed to the "twelve tribes scattered among the nations." James wrote to instruct and encourage Christians in the midst of persecution and personal trials. James is especially marked by its emphasis on a faith accompanied by good works and a lifestyle that is consistent in its faithfulness to Christ.

**468. First Peter.** This is the first of two letters from Peter written in Rome. He addressed it to the Gentiles of Asia Minor who were enduring severe persecution. It appears to be a letter meant to circulate; it deals with practical subjects of faith, hope, and love for everyday living. Although certain aspects of his style are rough, others are quite elegant and similar to classical Greek. This leads scholars to believe that Peter may have had a Greek amanuensis (someone to take dictation) named Silvanus (1 Peter 5:12).

**469. Second Peter.** In Peter's second letter (less elegantly written than 1 Peter) he began by pointing out that he did not have long to live and wanted to lay down the things most essential for his disciples to remember, urging them to grow in the knowledge of the truth. Near the end of this epistle, Peter made reference to some of Paul's letters.

**470. First John** is the first of three letters written by John. These three letters have notable similarities to his Gospel and the Book of Revelation. These letters speak out against the heresy of Gnosticism. The Gnostics taught that the body and this world are evil and that salvation came through special knowledge.

**471. Second John.** In this short but personal letter, John dealt with the problem of false teachers. He appeared to be counseling a particular congregation not to receive visiting teachers who proclaimed false teachings.

**472. Third John.** Ironically this letter dealt with the flip side of the problem covered in 2 John. In this case John wrote to a congregation that had been rejecting visiting teachers. Only here, the visiting teacher in question was true. Second and Third John are the two shortest books in the entire Bible.

**473. Jude,** like James, was a sibling of Jesus. His letter seemed to be written at a time when many of the apostles had already been martyred. He made references to their warnings about false teachers and Peter's and Paul's predictions. Jude made the point that these teachings had indeed reached projected proportions. Jude's writing sets the stage for the final book of the Bible.

**474. The Epistle of Jude** quotes from 1 Enoch 1:9 and the Assumption of Moses. Many Christians have not heard of these books because they were written before the time of the New Testament and were not accepted into the Canon of inspired Scripture by the Jewish or Christian communities. Yet Jude used them to make a point in his epistle.

**475. Apocalyptic writing** was a kind of code, a way of communicating that unbelieving enemies would not understand. A person who wrote such literature could encourage his readers to stand against the pagan state and predict its downfall under divine judgment, without fear of official reprisal. Modern readers often miss this aspect of the apocalyptic genre, just as the ancient pagans did.

It was designed to reveal its message to insiders in terms that an outsider could not understand.

**476. Revelation.** The longest of all the New Testament letters, "The Revelation to John" was addressed to seven specific communities, all of them located in Asia. Like Hebrews, this book was built upon quotations and allusions to Old Testament passages (hundreds of references). The line of the book is as follows: Goodness and evil wage a cataclysmic battle in which goodness wins the decisive victory. The practice of using bizarre conflicting images was a practiced style in ancient times. It was called "apocalyptic," so the book is sometimes called the Apocalypse instead of Revelation. The meaning is actually the same, only *apocalypse* comes from a Greek root, while *revelation* comes from a Latin root word.

**477. The identity and meaning of the beast** numbered 666 has deeply concerned Christians throughout history. Its symbolism has been assigned to Satanism in popular culture and to such notorious figures as Napoleon and Hitler. Some scholars believe that while Satan is a major player in Revelation, the meaning 666 was clear to the people of the time of its writing. In both Greek and Hebrew, letters doubled as numerals. One solution to the 666 puzzle? The number is produced by adding up the Hebrew letters of "Kaisar Neron," or Emperor Nero, which reaches an equivalent of the number 666.

**478. The extraordinary prophetic vision** of the second coming of Jesus and the last judgment were given while John was exiled on Patmos, an Aegean island used as a Roman penal colony. The author had been banished there for his preaching most likely during the reign of Roman Emperor Domitian (A.D. 81–96).

**479. Apocalypse** is the Greek name for the Book of Revelation. The word literally means "to unveil" or "to reveal something that has been hidden." The early church had numerous books claiming to reveal future events, and it wasn't until the fourth century that John's apocalypse was recognized as the one inspired version.

# 17

# A Savior, Which Is Christ the Lord

**480. Jesus Christ,** more than any other figure or historical happening mentioned, is the most important figure in the Bible. The Old Testament prophesies about his coming and his death, the New Testament sees him be born, establish a ministry, and eventually sacrifice himself for all who believe in him.

**481. Many incidences** in the Old Testament point to Christ: Abel's lamb was a type of Christ. So was Abraham's willing offering of his son, Isaac, for sacrifice. The Passover lamb in Egypt was a type of Christ. Even the scarlet cord the prostitute Rahab hung in her window was a symbol of Christ!

**482. "To him give all the prophets witness."** Truly, God had been telling his people about the coming Savior long before Jesus was ever born. Micah foretold Jesus' birth, Zechariah told of how he will eventually reign as King over all the earth. Joel described the day of judgment and what part Jesus will play in it.

**483. The New Testament** is the unraveling of all those prophesies and foretellings of the Old Testament. Jesus' birth is recorded in two Gospel books: Matthew and Luke.

**484. The Christmas story** reveals the depth of God's love to all humankind. Matthew's and Luke's Gospels tell the story of the virgin birth, the humble beginnings of Jesus, and the joyous celebration set off in heaven when Christ was born. Though missed by many, God allowed both great (the magi) and humble (the shepherds) to join in the celebration.

**485. The number of magi** who followed the star of Bethlehem is unknown. The Bible doesn't tell much about them. The Christian tradition that there were three kings did not arise until about seven hundred years after the event took place. Their legendary names—Balthasar, Melchior, and Caspar, in Western traditions—emerged much later. So did the story that one of them was black. Medieval Christians reasoned that the three kings must have come from the three continents, so one must have been African.

**486. The magi** did not come to the actual stable where Jesus was born. Their trip is thought to have taken place when Jesus was closer to two years old.

**487. Because Herod** ordered the slaughter of young Jewish children, Mary and Joseph fled to Egypt with the child Jesus. The Egypt in which Jesus found shelter was much different from the proud and mighty nation that his ancestors Abraham and Moses had known. The glory that had been Egypt was gone. The flourishing cities through which pharaohs once rode in pomp were decaying and the great pyramids and temples were crumbling.

**488. Symbolically the announcement of the angel** to the shepherds provides a counterpoint to the homage paid by the wealthy wise men. In New Testament times shepherds ranked low on the social register. The shepherds also served as a reminder that Jesus was coming as both the shepherd to the flock of Israel and as the sacrificial lamb that would take away the sins of the world.

**489. Joseph and Mary** returned from Egypt some time after the death of Herod in 4 B.C. and made their home in Nazareth, a town in Galilee. The name Nazareth is derived from Hebrew words that mean "consecrated people," because this town was noted for clinging to the ancient laws and customs of the Hebrews. Jesus' birthday is celebrated on December 25 now, but that wasn't always the case. For centuries a different calendar was used, and the date was in the spring.

**490. The baby Jesus** was like any other baby—he was human and had the same needs as babies do today. He cried to be held and fed, needed his diapers changed, and learned to talk like any other baby does.

**491. Though nativity scenes tell the story differently,** there were likely no animals present at Jesus' birth. The Bible makes no mention of camels, donkeys, cattle, or sheep. All these are cultural additions to the story that have been added through the ages.

**492. The shepherds weren't given a miraculous sign** to follow like the magi were two years later. The "star of the East" did not guide them. The angels told the shepherds to look for a baby wrapped in cloths and lying in a manger. Presumably this was an unusual sign in itself and the shepherds found Jesus with little difficulty.

**493. The Christmas story has undergone** cultural interpretation to such an extent that many people believe the Bible tells of Joseph asking the innkeeper if the baby can be born there. There is, however, no record of such a conversation occurring. Luke 2:7 simply states: "She wrapped him in cloths and placed him in a manger, because there was no room for them in the inn."

**494. Jesus did not receive his name,** which means "the Messiah" or "the Christ," until his eighth day when he was circumcised. The name had been given to Mary by the angel before she conceived, but the practice was to officially name the child when he was circumcised.

**495. At twelve years of age, Jesus** already demonstrated that he was aware of his lifework. His parents had taken him to the Passover feast in Jerusalem. When they left, they thought he was with them, but he had stayed behind in order to speak with the teachers at the temple.

**496. His ministry began when he was about thirty years of age.** John the Baptist was serving as a "voice in the wilderness" and calling the people to remember that their Savior was coming, that the time had come to repent. Jesus was baptized by John at the Jordan River.

**497. Satan tempted** Christ and tried to weaken the Savior's resolve, but Jesus stood firm in his mission. Christ's ministry would ultimately lead to his death, and though Satan's temptations would have saved him great pain, he was faithful to his heavenly Father.

**498. The Lord's preaching** took him all over the area for three years. He traveled throughout Galilee, Judea, and Samaria. He healed the sick and brought hope to many through miracles. He often spoke in parables to the people to help them better understand what his ministry was all about.

**499. Jesus spent much of his ministry life** in and around the Sea of Galilee. Galileans in Bible times were considered country hicks to the more cosmopolitan residents of Jerusalem. Jesus spoke primarily to the humble people who labored on the land and were familiar with the animals and plants around them. His parables are filled with images of the natural world.

**500. Jesus met all manner of people—and accepted them all** if they repented of their sins. Harlots, tax collectors, liars, cheats, the infirmed, and the diseased all received kind words, healing, and a message of hope. One such man was especially memorable.

**501. A rich tax collector called Zacchaeus** wanted to catch a glimpse of Jesus, but he had to climb a sycamore tree (Luke 19:4). This is an inferior kind of fig tree that has traditionally been a food of impoverished people in the Near East. Thus the rich man was forced to rely on the tree that was a symbol of poverty. Jesus did not harbor any love, however, for the proud and often conniving leaders of the Jewish faith who consistently misled the people.

**502. Obedience to laws** without a sense of mercy is an action empty of spiritual value. Several times Jesus quoted the prophets who had said, "God desires mercy more than sacrifice." He reserved a special anger for the scribes and Pharisees, who might loosely be called "lawyers." Matthew's term for Pharisees is *hypocrites,* a term in Greek that applied to actors or people who were pretenders. They were people who said one thing but did another.

**503. The Pharisees** were a group of Jewish clerics who felt that their strict obedience to Jewish traditions set them apart from the rest of the pagan culture. Their name means "the separated ones." They were intolerant of anyone considered ritually unclean and persecuted many people. Their reliance on rules made them appear pious to the masses, but Jesus criticized them for having an outward show of piety while neglecting the fact that inwardly they were proud, pompous sinners.

**504. The Sadducees** were the Jewish aristocracy who rather enjoyed the artistic and political advantages that came from being allied to the Roman Empire. During Christ's life they controlled the high Jewish council, called the Sanhedrin, but they were haughty and pompous and generally disliked by the common people.

**505. Jesus called special helpers to his aid** in order to preach and teach and minister to the people. There were twelve helpers in all—Simon Peter, Andrew, James, John, Philip, Bartholomew, Thomas, Matthew, James, Thaddaeus, Simon the Zealot, and Judas Iscariot.

**506. The words** *disciple* **and** *apostle* are often used interchangeably but mean quite different things. The word *disciples* means "learners" or "students." The disciples of Jesus were those who listened to Jesus, followed him, and even taught what Jesus taught. An apostle, from the Greek *apostolos,* for "one who is sent out," generally means a messenger of the gospel. The author of Luke used the word *apostle* specifically for the twelve disciples who had been companions of Jesus, were witnesses of the resurrection, and eventually became leaders of the church.

**507. The name Mary,** derived from the Greek form of the common Hebrew *Miriam,* the name of the sister of Moses, is the name of three different women in the life of Jesus. His mother Mary only made a few appearances in the Gospel accounts, but she was at the foot of the cross with John. Mary the sister of Martha and Lazarus was a close friend of Jesus. Jesus healed Mary Magdalene (or Mary of Magdala, a town near Tiberias) by casting out the demons within her. She then became a devoted follower of Christ.

**508. To the devout Jews who accepted Jesus,** he was the promised Savior who fulfilled the word expressed in their Scriptures of a coming "Messiah" or "anointed one" from the line of David who would deliver the children of Israel and usher in a new age of peace under God's rule. Though he was later called the "Christ," this is not a name but a title. *Christos* comes from the Greek meaning "anointed one" or "Messiah."

**509. Hebrew was still the language** of the places of worship, but outside of them the people spoke a dialect known as Aramaic. They also carried on conversations in Greek. It was not the classical language of Homer and the heroes, but a dialect known as Koine, the language in which the bulk of the New Testament was written. Undoubtedly Jesus learned to speak all three languages.

**510. The "eye of a needle"** was the phrase Jesus used in Mark 10:25 when he said, "It is easier for a camel to go through the eye of a needle than for a rich man to enter the kingdom of God." Those words must have shocked his original audience, who had thought that prosperity was a sign of God's blessing. In recent years some people have tried to identify a particular gate into Jerusalem as "the eye of the needle," thereby missing Christ's main point: Someone committed to worldly wealth is probably not as interested in heavenly gain.

**511. Jesus was not alone in works of healing.** Just as other men claimed messiahship to attract political followers, numerous wonder-workers and healers wandered the Roman Empire in that day. Jesus even referred to others who were healing in his time. The Jewish Talmud discusses several wonder-working rabbis of Jesus' time. But none made the claim that Jesus' followers made— that he had the ability to raise the dead and had done so on three occasions with witnesses.

**512. Jesus was well-received by the people** as long as he was performing miracles and teaching, but they did not look to him as the King of Kings. Sadly they were looking for an earthly king instead of a heavenly one. As a result their love for Jesus was short-lived.

**513. Jesus took three of his most trusted disciples** up on a mountain, where they experienced an extraordinary event. While the disciples watched, Jesus was miraculously "transfigured." His physical being was transformed, and the figures of Moses and Elijah, the two great prophets of Judaism, stood beside him. The disciples also heard the voice of God saying Jesus was God's beloved Son. The accounts all say Jesus' face shone as Moses' did when he encountered God on Mount Sinai in Exodus.

**514. As Christ rode a donkey** into Jerusalem, he was hailed by the people with palm leaves and shouts of "Hosanna!" The people celebrated him as their king. They did not want the greatest gift that Christ offered and that they needed most. They wanted freedom from the Romans and a nation of their own instead, and thought Christ brought that, despite the many warnings and explanations given of his ministry.

**515. Satan provoked Judas to betray Jesus,** as it is stated in the Gospel of John. The treachery of Judas has provoked some speculation over motives, including the notion that he might have been an anti-Roman zealot who was disappointed that Jesus had not proved to be the rebel leader many were expecting. The Gospel of Mark tells how Judas went to the chief priests to betray Jesus before being offered a bribe, suggesting that he had some other motive besides money. Matthew specifically states that Judas asked how much he would be given, and he was paid "thirty pieces of silver" in fulfillment of ancient Hebrew prophecy.

**516. The Last Supper was a preparation for Jesus himself** as he readied himself for the end, which he knew was near. Judas Iscariot was even confronted by Christ at the table. The Lord celebrated a final supper with his disciples, his most trusted companions. This special dinner was given to Christians in order to remember the sacrifice Jesus made for his people.

**517. The words "Take and eat: this is my body,"** and "This is my blood of the covenant, which is poured out for many for the forgiveness of sins" (Matt. 26:26, 28) are part of a sacrament of the Christian church that originated with the Last Supper. Communion is based on the events of the Last Supper and serves as one of two main sacraments in the Christian church to this day.

**518. After the Last Supper,** Jesus spent his last night of freedom in the Garden of Gethsemane on the slopes of the Mount of Olives. The name means "olive presses." In Jesus' time the Mount of Olives was covered with a luxuriant growth of these trees, and the inhabitants of Jerusalem often rested there to seek relief from the sun.

**519. "Today—yes, tonight—**before the rooster crows twice you yourself will disown me three times" (Mark 14:30). On the way to Gethsemane, Jesus told his disciple Peter this prophecy. The roosters first crowed about midnight, and they were so punctual that Roman soldiers used the sound as a signal for changing the guard. The roosters crowed a second time about three o'clock in the morning, which awakened the second watch of soldiers.

**520. Many first-century Jews died, just like Jesus,** on a cross. Some estimates for the number of Jews crucified in this time for a variety of crimes run as high as one hundred thousand. But this was not at the hand of other Jews. Crucifixion was exclusive to the Romans, and it was an extreme penalty generally reserved for cases of runaway slaves or rebellion against Rome. An uprising of slaves against Rome led by the gladiator-slave Spartacus in 71 B.C. resulted in some six thousand crucifixions. Bodies were left to decompose as a grim warning.

**521. Gall** is mentioned several times in the Bible. It refers to the juice of a poisonous and bitter plant, but there is no way of knowing exactly which plant. The best guess is the poison hemlock, the plant that poisoned Socrates and served medicinally as a sedative. Hemlock was considered a plant of ill omen and associated with witches and evil spirits.

**522. The Seven Last Utterances** are the final words spoken by Christ while on the cross. The four Gospels reveal different phrases, but grouped together they include: (1) "Today you will be with me in paradise" (spoken to the thief next to him). (2) "My God, my God, why have you forsaken me?" (3) "Father, forgive them, for they know not what they do." (4) "I thirst." (5) "Woman, behold your son. Son, behold your mother" (spoken to Mary and the disciple John). (6) "It is finished." (7) "Into your hands I commit my spirit."

**523. "A mixture of myrrh and aloes,** about a hundred pound weight" was brought after the crucifixion. "Then took they the body of Jesus, and wound it in linen clothes with the spices, as the manner of the Jews is to bury" (John 19:39–40 KJV). Myrrh was one of the main ingredients used in the purification of the dead.

**524. The linen in which Jesus' body** was wound was made from flax, the oldest textile fiber known. In the ancient world there were different grades of linen. Fine linen was used in the cloths of the rich, for curtain hangings in the temple, and even for sails of Phoenician trading ships. The poor people, however, wore only ordinary coarse linen. The Bible did not specify what type of linen Jesus was wound in.

**525. The death of Jesus at Golgotha** must have had no more significance to the Romans than the deaths of the thousands of other Jews they crucified at that time. Yet soon the whole ancient world heard about Jesus. His disciples carried his teaching to the farthest outpost of the Roman Empire.

**526. Yet to one Roman, Christ's death did have significance.** The Roman centurion who watched Christ die said, "Surely this man was the Son of God!" when he saw the sun darken and felt the earth quake at Jesus' death.

**527. The resurrection of Jesus** is the central story to all Christianity. After dying on the cross, being wrapped in a burial shroud, and being interred in a sealed tomb, Jesus rose from the dead—conquering death and offering the hope of eternal life to all who believe in him.

**528. After Jesus was resurrected,** he appeared several times to various disciples. His resurrection fulfilled every prophecy he and all the early prophets had made concerning the Savior of the world. Though some doubted, many believed and were brought to a saving understanding that Jesus was truly their Savior and the King of Kings.

**529. Jesus commissioned his followers** to preach the gospel to all people. His call to them brought the disciples and other faithful followers to the beginning of the church. And through a history of almost two thousand years, the church has experienced persecution, misery, and separation. Yet never has it died and never will it fall, despite what might happen, for Christ is the head of his church. And his kingdom cannot fail!

**530. Christ ascended into heaven,** on a cloud, to be with the Father and to "sit at the right hand of God" until the time of his second coming. He will come again at "the last days" as the Bible writers prophesied. His message remains today for all who will believe in him and trust him as their personal Savior.

# 18

# Miracles of Amazing Proportions

**531. Biblical miracles** are found in both the Old and New Testaments. Many show God's power over nature while other miracles are a sign of his mercy and love for those who fear him. These events are supernatural and can only be the work of God.

**532. Miracles demonstrate God's hand** intervening in earthly affairs in extraordinary ways. New Testament miracles tend to be "personal" miracles, as opposed to miracles affecting the entire nation, such as the plagues on Egypt or the crossing of the Red Sea. Apart from his own miraculous birth, resurrection, and the transfiguration, Jesus performed more than thirty-five miracles in the Gospels.

## OLD TESTAMENT MIRACLES

**533. The flood** is an example of a miracle of nature. Certainly it was a judgment against the world, but it was no less than a sign of God's power and dominion. He caused it to rain so hard and so fast and so long (forty days) that every living thing on the whole earth was swallowed up in a gigantic flood.

**534. Noah's surviving in the ark** during the flood is an example of God's provision and mercy for the one man and his family who did not die in the flood. That this man was able to build the ark and then fill it with animals and find food for all of them is an amazing feat—too amazing to be possible without divine intervention.

**535. Sarah delivered a healthy baby boy** when she was well past her childbearing years. Her husband, Abraham, was already a centenarian, and she had given up hope of having a child. Yet God had promised them a son to fulfill the covenant.

**536. The burning bush.** The first clear miracle recorded in the Bible is Moses' encounter with God, described in Exodus 3. That passage describes Moses, who was living as a shepherd in Midian, seeing a bush that was on fire but did not burn up. As Moses approached, God called him by name, told him that he was standing on holy ground, and announced that he would be sent to free the Israelite slaves in Egypt. While earlier passages describe things like the miraculous growth of Jacob's herd of sheep or the hand of God on Joseph's life, this is the first recorded instance of a clearly supernatural act.

**537. Aaron's staff becomes a snake.** When Moses and Aaron approached Pharaoh in Exodus 7, they threw a wooden staff to the floor, and it miraculously turned into a snake. After Pharaoh's magicians appeared to duplicate that feat, Aaron's staff/snake swallowed all the magicians' snakes—a sign of God's supernatural power being greater than that of man's magical power.

**538. The ten plagues.** In an attempt to free his people from slavery, Moses revealed to Pharaoh that ten plagues would hit Egypt: water turning to blood, frogs, gnats, flies, cattle disease, boils, hail, locusts, darkness, and the death of all firstborn males. While there are natural explanations for all ten, the occurrence of them all together, along with the fact that Moses predicted them, certainly categorize them as a special act of God.

**539. The pillar of fire and the parting of the Red Sea.** Exodus 14 describes the flight of the Israelites from Egypt. Pharaoh's armies, chasing them, were kept from approaching the Israelite camp by a protective pillar of fire. The Red Sea then opened up, allowing the Israelites to cross the sea "on dry land." When the Egyptians tried to follow, the sea closed over them, killing them all. The pillar then guided the Israelites through the wilderness—a cloud by day, and fire by night.

**540. Manna from heaven.** While the Israelites lived in the wilderness, God miraculously provided them with bread from heaven that would appear on the ground each morning like dew. Exodus 16:31 describes it as tasting "like wafers made with honey," and the Jews referred to it as manna, which literally means, "What is it?"

**541. Water from the rock.** When the people in the wilderness were thirsty, Moses was instructed by God to strike a rock with his stick. Exodus 17 records that Moses did this in full view of the elders, and water poured forth from the rock, quenching the thirst of the Israelites.

**542. The budding of Aaron's staff.** In an attempt to prove that Aaron had a special place of leadership, Moses gathered the walking staffs of each tribal leader and placed them in a tent before the Lord. The next morning Aaron's staff had sprouted, budded, blossomed, and produced almonds, according to Numbers 17:8. The staff was kept in front of the people, as a sign of God's choice of leaders.

**543. The bronze snake.** Numbers 21 tells how God sent venomous snakes among the people as a discipline for complaining. After many Israelites died, God told Moses to make a bronze snake and put it on a high pole. Anyone who was bitten could simply turn and look at the snake, and they would be saved. Just as the bronze snake was lifted up and offered life to those who would believe and turn toward it, Christ was lifted up and offers the free gift of salvation to all who believe.

**544. The walls of Jericho.** While most Old Testament miracles were confined to the lives of Moses, Elijah, Elisha, and Daniel, one of the few other supernatural events occurs in Joshua 5–6. Rather than attacking the city of Jericho, the armies of Israel followed God's command to march around the city walls and blow trumpets. After doing this for a week, they gave a great shout and the walls of Jericho simply fell down in front of them. Recent archaeology of the site has shown that the walls did, indeed, fall outward—a strange occurrence, since walls were generally pushed inward by invading armies.

**545. Gideon's fleece.** Another Old Testament miracle is recorded in Judges 6. Gideon, chosen by God to lead Israel's armies, needed a sign that God was really on his side. He laid a fleece on the ground one night and asked the Lord to let it be wet with dew the next morning, even though the ground was dry. God did just that. The next night Gideon laid the fleece and asked that it would be dry while the ground was wet. Again God acted. This miracle has led to people talking about "laying out a fleece" when they want to test something or someone.

**546. Fed by ravens.** The prophet Elijah, after proclaiming a drought, hid in the Kerith Ravine. First Kings 17 records that God sent ravens with bread and meat to him every morning and evening, sustaining him through the difficult times.

**547. Multiplying flour and oil.** When Elijah asked the widow of Zarephath to make him a cake during the drought, she replied that she and her son were about to die of starvation. However, Elijah told her that if she made him a meal, her jar of flour would never run out and her jar of oil would never run dry. First Kings 17:15–16 records that the widow's jars were miraculously filled each day.

**548. Raising the widow's son.** When the widow of Zarephath's son died, Elijah took the boy in his arms, went into an upper room, and cried out to the Lord, "O Lord my God, let this boy's life return to him!" (1 Kings 17:21). God raised the boy to life—presaging a miracle Jesus Christ would perform hundreds of years later.

**549. Fire on Mount Carmel.** One of the best stories in Scripture takes place in 1 Kings 18, when Elijah did battle with 450 prophets of Baal. Placing a bull on an altar on top of Mount Carmel, he challenged the prophets to make fire come down and consume the sacrifice. When they failed, he taunted them, suggesting that their god must be asleep or away on a trip. Elijah then had water poured on the bull, stepped forward, and said a short prayer: "Let it be known today that you are God in Israel and that I am your servant." Fire suddenly came from heaven and burned up the sacrifice—leading the crowd watching to prostrate themselves before God, then turn and slaughter the false priests.

**550. Chariots of fire.** Second Kings 2 records that Elijah did not die, but was taken up to heaven in a chariot of fire pulled by horses of fire. Those same chariots appeared later in Elisha's life, when the Aramean armies came to capture him. Though Elisha's servant was afraid for his life, God opened his eyes and helped him to see that they were surrounded by chariots of fire sent by God. In response to that vision, Elisha struck the entire Aramean army blind.

**551. Oil aplenty.** When a widow asked Elisha for help to pay her creditors, the prophet instructed her to ask neighbors for their empty jars. After collecting the jars, she was to pour oil from her small oil pot into the jars. She kept pouring and pouring, miraculously multiplying her oil until all the jars were filled. The widow then sold the oil and paid her debts.

**552. Raising the Shunammite's son.** When a childless woman invited Elisha to stay with her, then prepared his room and all his meals, the prophet announced she would soon become pregnant and have a son. She did, but the boy died from an internal problem a few years later. Second Kings 4 reveals that Elisha went to see the body, lay down on top of him, and raised the boy to life.

**553. Feeding the multitudes.** Elisha took twenty loaves of barley bread and divided them among a hundred men. According to 2 Kings 4:42–44, the Lord multiplied the bread so that everyone had their fill, and there was bread left over. Jesus would later do a similar miracle, feeding five thousand, recorded in Matthew 14.

**554. Naaman healed of leprosy.** When the commander of Syria's armies came down with leprosy, his wife encouraged him to visit Elisha. The prophet told Naaman to wash seven times in the Jordan River. Though he was skeptical, Naaman did as he was told and was miraculously cured of his disease. Second Kings 5:15 records his response: "Now I know that there is no God in all the world except in Israel."

**555. An axhead floats.** Second Kings 6 tells the story of a workman with a borrowed ax cutting some trees, when the axhead fell into some water. Elisha cut a stick, threw it into the water, and the iron axhead floated to the top.

**556. Nebuchadnezzar's dream.** The king of Babylon, who conquered Jerusalem and carried off its citizenry into exile, had a strange dream that none of his wise men could interpret. But the prophet Daniel, a young Jew selected to serve in Nebuchadnezzar's court, asked God to help him understand the dream. Not only did God reveal the dream to Daniel, but the Lord gave him the meaning of the dream—which accurately revealed what would happen to future kingdoms.

**557. The fiery furnace.** When Daniel's three friends—Shadrach, Meshach, and Abednigo—refused to bow down to an idol, the king of Babylon had them thrown into a fiery furnace. The furnace was so hot that even the soldiers leading them toward it were killed, but the three followers of God were miraculously saved. When the king looked into the furnace, he saw not only the three men but a fourth man, who looked like "the Son of God." Recognizing it as a miracle, he issued a decree that no one was to slander the God of Israel.

**558. The writing is on the wall.** Daniel 5 records that when the loathsome King Belshazzar threw a drunken party and used sacred cups that had been brought from the temple in Jerusalem, the fingers of a human hand suddenly appeared and wrote a message on a wall: "Numbered. Weighed. Divided." Though none of the king's astrologers could divine the meaning, Daniel could. He told the king that God had judged Belshazzar and found him wanting, so his kingdom would be taken away that very night. That is exactly what happened.

**559. Daniel in the lion's den.** When King Darius decreed that anyone found praying to God would be killed, Daniel went into his room, opened the shutters, and prayed loudly to the Lord. Darius reluctantly had Daniel thrown into a lion's den, but God shut the mouths of the lions and he was preserved without a scratch. The court members who had plotted against Daniel were then thrown into the den and devoured.

**560. Jonah and the whale.** The last miracle recorded in the Old Testament involves the reluctant prophet Jonah who, while attempting to run away from God, was caught in a horrible storm and thrown into the sea in the sailors' attempt to pacify their gods. He was swallowed by a great fish, survived for three days, then was coughed up onto the shore. Upon reaching the intended city of Nineveh, Jonah preached repentance, and the pagans there turned to God (much to Jonah's disgust).

## NEW TESTAMENT MIRACLES

**561. The virgin birth.** No doubt the first miraculous event recorded in the New Testament is the birth of Jesus Christ. Mary, a virgin, was "found to be with child through the Holy Spirit," according to Matthew 1:18. Several other miracles surrounded that birth, including the striking dumb of Zechariah in Luke 1, the angels' appearance to the shepherds in Luke 2, and the star which led the magi to visit in Matthew 2.

**562. Water into wine.** The first recorded miracle of Jesus occurs in John 2, when Christ was attending a wedding in the city of Cana and the hosts ran out of wine. Jesus requested six large jars to be filled with water, and they then miraculously turned into fine wine. As John records, "He thus revealed his glory, and his disciples put their faith in him."

**563. Healing.** One of the things Christ was most known for was his ability to heal the sick. Matthew 4:23–24 records that "Jesus went throughout Galilee . . . healing every disease and sickness among the people. News about him spread all over Syria, and people brought to him all who were ill with various diseases, those suffering severe pain, the demon-possessed, those having seizures, and the paralyzed, and he healed them." The sick included lepers, paralytics, and those with internal bleeding.

**564. A man born blind.** Certainly one of the most amazing miracles of Jesus was the healing of a man born blind in John 9. Christ made some mud with his saliva, rubbed it on the man's eyes, and instructed him to wash in a nearby pool. Upon doing so the man received his sight. Jewish leaders denounced him as a fraud, but when questioned, the man responded, "One thing I do know. I was blind and now I see!"

**565. The centurion's servant.** Since Roman conquerors were hated by most Jewish citizens, it was generally forbidden for a Jew to enter a Roman's home. Thus when a God-fearing Roman centurion told Jesus that his servant was ill, he informed the Lord that Jesus didn't have to enter his home to perform the healing. Instead Christ could do it from a distance. Marveling at the man's faith, Jesus replied, "I have not found anyone in Israel with such great faith" (Matt. 8:10). Before the centurion could get home, the servant was healed.

**566. Jesus calms the storm.** Matthew 8 relates the story of Jesus asleep in a boat when a violent storm arose. When the disciples, fearing they would drown, awakened the Lord, he simply rebuked the winds and the waves, making them calm.

**567. Raising the dead.** In Matthew 9, Jesus tells a crowd of mourners that a ruler's young daughter is not dead but asleep. Though the mourners laughed at him, Jesus proceeds to raise her from the dead. Luke 7 also tells of Jesus raising the dead, this time a widow's son. And John 11 records the raising of Lazarus, which was witnessed by a crowd of people.

**568. Feeding the multitudes.** After preaching to a large crowd, the disciples encouraged Christ to send the people away so that they could find something to eat. Instead the Lord had them gather their food—five loaves of bread and two fish—and proceeded to feed five thousand people.

**569. Walking on water.** After his disciples had sailed off in a boat to the other side of a lake, the disciples watched Jesus walk out to them on the waves. Peter asked to join him, and also walked on water for a short time. But Matthew notes that as soon as Peter took his eyes off the Lord and began to look at the waves, he began to sink. Christ helped Peter back into the boat—prompting the disciples to say, "Truly you are the Son of God."

**570. The transfiguration.** A few days before his death, Jesus took Peter, James, and John up to a high mountain. There he was "transfigured" before them. His face "shone like the sun, and his clothes became as white as the light." Moses and Elijah, two of the handful of miracle workers in Scripture, then appeared with Jesus, and the voice of God announced, "This is my Son, whom I love; with him I am well pleased" (Matt. 17:5).

**571. The tearing of the veil.** Matthew 27:51 records an important miracle that took place during Christ's death on the cross: "At that moment the curtain of the temple was torn in two from top to bottom." The tearing of that curtain, which created a barrier between the worship area and the holy of holies where God dwelt, meant that man was no longer to be separated from God.

**572. The resurrection.** The greatest of all miracles in the Christian faith is the fact that Jesus rose from the dead, conquering death and sin. The evidence for the resurrection as a historical fact (the empty tomb, the Roman guard, the eyewitness reports of those who were there, the lack of any other explanation) is overwhelming.

**573. Apostles heal a cripple.** In the apostolic age some of the followers of Christ had the power to do miracles. Acts 3 records Peter and John healing a beggar who had been crippled since birth, and Acts 5:12 notes that "the apostles performed many miraculous signs and wonders among the people."

**574. Ananias and Sapphira.** The early church encouraged members to take care of one another. One couple, Ananias and Sapphira, schemed to sell some property and give some of the money away but then deceive the church by keeping some of it for themselves. When they stood before the leadership, God struck both Ananias and Sapphira dead.

**575. Peter's escape from prison.** When Peter was arrested for preaching the gospel, he was held in prison, bound to a soldier on either side. But Acts 12 relates that late one night Peter was awakened by an angel, his chains simply fell off, and the gates before him miraculously opened by themselves. He walked to freedom . . . while the guards who were supposed to be keeping watch over him were later executed.

# 19

# Speaking in Pictures

**576. The parable of the sower,** found in Matthew 13, likens sharing the gospel to a farmer scattering seed. Seed sown on the path is eaten by birds—which the Lord explains is similar to what occurs when a hearer doesn't understand the message. Satan snatches it away, so that it cannot have an impact on the hearer's life. Seed scattered on rocky soil sprouts, but it dies because it cannot set its roots—this is likened to someone who initially believes the gospel but falls away from the faith due to persecution. Some seeds grow but are choked out by thorns—a depiction of the person whose belief is undermined by worldly concerns. But the good seed that grows is like the individual who hears the gospel, understands it, and chooses to follow Christ.

**577. The parable of the weeds** also tells the story of a farmer sowing seeds, but an enemy sows weeds among the wheat. When it sprouts, a servant asks the farmer if he should pull them up. The farmer replies, "No, because while you are pulling the weeds, you may root up the wheat with them. Let both grow together until the harvest" (Matt. 13:29). Jesus later explains that he is the good seed, the weeds are the sons of evil, spread by the enemy Satan, and the field is the world. The harvest represents the end of time, when God will bring his people into his house, but send those who reject him to judgment.

**578. The parable of the new wine in old wineskins,** found in Matthew 9:16–17, describes the new life Jesus brings. This new life cannot be confined by old forms—or by hardened hearts. Jesus' meaning was clear: to embrace the special gift he brought, a person had to be born again, to become a new form, because the old one would burst and be ruined by the message of Jesus.

**579. The parable of the wise and wicked servants** discusses what faithful servants (believers) should be doing while their master (Jesus) is away. A wise servant who is left in charge of the other servants will make sure they are being taken care of and doing their work. The foolish servant will assume he can do as he likes since the master will be staying away a long time. He will beat the other laborers and become drunk. Yet the master will return unexpectedly and find out who has acted wisely and who has acted foolishly. The foolish servant will be cast into a dreadful place for not honoring the master while he is away.

**580. The parable of the sheep and the goats** is a picture of what will happen when Christ returns. Sheep symbolize believers; goats symbolize unbelievers. The sheep will be parted from the goats with a final destination of heaven. The goats will be sent to hell, the place of eternal punishment.

**581. The parable of the growing seed** is only found in one of the Gospels of the New Testament—Mark. The parable describes how the kingdom of God is like a seed that is scattered into the ground and eventually sprouts and grows and produces grain. It does this with no help or direction. The seed's power to grow itself is likened to the power of the gospel message: It has its own mysterious power.

**582. The parable of the watchful porter** is a reminder that no one knows the exact return of Christ. Believers are to be ready, to stand at attention like an attentive porter would at the door of a building, to not let down their guard as they wait for Christ's return.

**583. The parable of the two debtors** likens debtors to sinners. In this very short parable from Luke, there are two debtors. One owes a small amount of money to a lender, the other ten times the amount of the first debtor. If the lender forgives both of them, Jesus asks, who will be more thankful? The obvious answer is the debtor with the larger amount of debt. The same concept holds true for sinners. Whether large or small, Christ forgives, but those with more to be forgiven will be more thankful. This parable was told after Jesus' feet were anointed by a former prostitute. The Pharisee sitting at the table was convinced Jesus wouldn't let such a sinner touch him if he only knew her past. Jesus' parable speaks directly to the heart issue.

**584. The parable of the good samaritan** tells the story of a man who was beaten by robbers and left for dead. Though a passing priest and temple worker refused to help the victim, a despised Samaritan stopped, assisted the man, and agreed to pay for all costs in his recuperation. The story shows that God's love moves beyond social prejudice.

**585. The parable of the barren fig tree** is a picture of how eternity will not wait forever for nonbelievers to make up their minds. In the story the owner of a vineyard tells the steward to cut down a fig tree that hasn't yielded fruit in three years. Thinking he has allowed an ample amount of time, the owner is frustrated and sees no point in using up soil to nourish it. Yet the steward asks for one more year to fertilize the fig—perhaps the steward is Christ interceding on our behalf!

**586. The parable of the lowest seat at the feast** likens the seating arrangement to how Christians are to behave on earth. They are to humble themselves now in order to be exalted later. At a feast it is wise to take a seat in a lower position and then be asked to move up to a more exalted position rather than exalting oneself first and then being asked to move down by the host. This is an often-repeated theme in the Bible: Believers are to be humble and not seek out positions of exaltation.

**587. The parable of the great banquet** is a reminder that not everyone will enter the kingdom of heaven. Though all are invited, many will reject the invitation and be lost. The story describes a gracious host who plans a large banquet and sends invitations to many people. But on the day of the banquet, those who are invited make excuses and don't come. The owner then sends for the poor, the lame, those who are in need. He will not force anyone to come into the banquet hall. Rather it is a matter of accepting an invitation.

**588. The parable of the mustard seed** likens the kingdom of heaven to the smallest seed known in that part of the world. Though the seed is tiny, it grows to a great height. In the same way, though the church started small, it would grow rapidly and become a worldwide force throughout the rest of history.

**589. In the parable of the yeast,** Jesus describes the kingdom of heaven as being like a small amount of yeast that gets mixed into a large amount of flour, permeating all the dough. Once the process of leavening begins, it cannot be stopped. Similarly once the good news of the gospel took hold in the world, there would be no stopping it. (In a later passage, Christ would warn against the evil yeast of the Pharisees, which could also permeate lives.)

**590. The parables of the hidden treasure and the pearl** both compare the gospel message to something of great value. Just as a man sells all he has in order to purchase the field with hidden treasure or the fine pearl, Jesus would give all he had—even his own life—in order to provide redemption for his people.

**591. The parable of the net** states that the kingdom of God is like a net that catches all kinds of fish. When the net is full, it is pulled on shore and the good fish are separated from the bad fish. Jesus explains that the net and sorting represent the action that will take place at the end of time, when Christ will remove the righteous from the unrighteous, sending believers to heaven and unbelievers to hell.

**592. The parable of the lost sheep,** in Matthew 18, is one of the sweetest stories of Jesus. In it he tells of a loving shepherd caring for one hundred sheep. If one gets lost, he will leave the ninety-nine to go find the one that is missing. In the same way, God is concerned about each person and he doesn't want anyone to be lost.

**593. The parable of the lost coin** likens a poor woman's rejoicing when finding a lost coin to the rejoicing in heaven when a sinner repents and turns to God. This parable can be found in Luke 15.

**594. The parable of the unmerciful servant** relates the story of a man who owes a great debt to his master. Falling on his knees, he pleads for mercy and it is granted. But moments later the servant sees a man who owes him a small amount and has him thrown into debtors' prison. When the master hears of this, he is outraged and has the servant arrested and punished until he can pay back his entire debt. Forgiveness should be in direct proportion to the amount forgiven—since the servant had been forgiven much, he should in turn forgive others. Since Christians have been forgiven for all their sins, they should in turn be willing to forgive the failings of others.

**595. The parable of the workers in the vineyard,** found in Matthew 20, tells the story of a landowner hiring workers to help in his fields. Some are hired in the morning, some at noon, and others near the end of the day, but they are all paid the same amount. Jesus used the parable to explain that rewards are under the sovereign control of God. Some prominent people will be demoted while some lowly people are exalted. The Lord's evaluation is all that matters in the final accounting of our lives.

**596. The parable of two sons** is about a father asking two boys to work in a vineyard. One says he will, but fails to go. The other says he won't, but does anyway. The one who eventually obeyed was righteous—a point Christ used to explain why prostitutes and tax collectors who turn to God will make it into heaven, while the Pharisees and religious leaders will not because they have not repented and believed.

**597. The parable of the tenants** may have been Christ's most powerful story. In Matthew 21 he tells of a careful landowner who rents out his vineyard. When he sends servants to collect the rent, the tenants beat them. Then he sends his own son, whom the tenants kill. Jesus used this illustration to depict a loving God caring for Israel yet being rejected by them. Eventually God sent his own Son, whom they would crucify. The result is that the kingdom of God would be taken from Israel. The religious leaders of the day, completely misunderstanding Christ's meaning, were enraged by the parable.

**598. The parable of the wise and foolish builders** contrasts a wise man who builds his house on a rock foundation with a foolish man who builds his house on sand. When a storm comes, the house on sand falls apart, while the house built on rock stands firm. In other words, the quality of the foundation determines the strength of the building. The firm foundation represents Christ's work of transforming lives from the inside out, contrasted with the Pharisees' religion, which relies on a merely outward appearance of righteousness. This parable, following a story about choosing which fruit to eat and which road to walk, reveals that there is always a wise choice that leads to God and a foolish choice that leads away from him.

**599. The parable of the wedding banquet** tells the story of a king trying to invite people to his son's celebration. Since the invitations are ignored or rejected by most, he angrily sends his army to punish those who snubbed him and invite people off the street to fill the wedding hall. The parable illustrates that Israel had rejected their Messiah, so Gentiles would be welcomed into the kingdom of God. An interesting detail is that one guest is expelled for not wearing wedding clothes that were given by the king—an illustration that we must not only respond to God outwardly, but inwardly by appropriating what God provides.

**600. The parable of the ten virgins,** found in Matthew 25, pictures Israel as ten virgins awaiting the return of the bridegroom. The wedding custom of the day called for the groom to return to his home leading a procession, and the image is that of Christ returning from heaven with his bride, the church. Preparation for the banquet is necessary, but five of the virgins have failed to prepare by bringing enough oil. They leave to shop for oil, and by the time they get back, the feast is in progress and they are denied admission. The image is that Israel is unprepared, though they should know that the Messiah is coming.

**601. The parable of the talents** is the story of a master entrusting three servants with various amounts of money to invest while he is away. Upon his return two have invested wisely and are praised. The third has hidden his money and is rebuked. His words and actions reveal a lack of faith in the master. The point of the parable is that God's people must serve him while he is away.

**602. The parable of the lamp** reminds us that no one lights a lamp and then hides it. Instead we use a lamp to illuminate the darkness. In the same way, we have not been given the truth of the gospel in order to keep it a secret, but to share it with others.

**603. The parable of the prodigal son** is one of the most well-told stories in Scripture. A father has two sons, one of whom demands his inheritance, leaves town, and wastes the money on foolish pleasures. The other son stays at home, working with his father. When the profligate son decides to return, the father rejoices, while his brother grouses about his father's response. Christ's point in telling the story was that not only is everyone welcome in God's family, but we should all rejoice when a lost soul repents and enters into fellowship with God.

**604. The parable of the rich fool,** related in Luke 12, tells of a wealthy man who builds bigger and bigger barns, promising himself that he will soon be able to take life easy. God's response is clear: "You fool! This very night your life will be demanded from you." Life is more important than hoarding material things. The rich fool's wealth would do him no good in eternity.

**605. The parable of the shrewd manager** is one of the more difficult parables to understand. A financial manager, in danger of losing his job, does favors for some of the people who owe money to his master. The master then praises the manager for acting shrewdly. The point is not that it's good to be dishonest, but that it was good the manager had planned ahead—in essence, he had used material goods for future benefits.

**606. The parable of the rich man and Lazarus,** in Luke 16, relates a story of a wealthy man dying and going to hell, while a poor man dies and goes to heaven. The initial point Christ was making was that material wealth has nothing to do with spiritual righteousness. But there is more to the story. When the rich man asks to go back and warn his living brothers, his request is rejected— a suggestion from the Lord that people will always be asking for more signs, even though they've already been given more than enough information that Jesus is the Christ.

**607. The parable of the persistent widow** tells of a woman seeking justice from an unjust judge. Though he routinely refuses to hear her case, the woman's persistence finally wears him down, and she gains justice. Jesus interpreted the parable by saying, "Listen to what the unjust judge says. And will not God bring about justice for his chosen ones, who cry out to him day and night?" (Luke 18:6–7).

**608. The parable of the pharisee and the tax collector** is perhaps the most touching story Christ told. A self-righteous priest stands before God and offers a prayer of thanks that he is not like the tax collector. But the tax collector is too humbled to even look up to God and pleads with the Lord to forgive him for his sins. Jesus' point is that we dare not trust in our own righteousness or compare ourselves to others in order to be justified. Instead we must humble ourselves before God in order to find forgiveness and gain his righteousness.

# 20

# A Church Begins

**609. Until the Book of Acts,** the Bible primarily belonged to the Jewish people. Of the many radical elements of Jesus' message, one of the most radical was that he meant for it to apply to Gentiles (non-Jews) as well as Jews. When Jesus told his apostles to go to the ends of the world, he really meant it. This brisk narrative begins in Jerusalem and ends in Rome, symbolizing how Jesus took the faith of ancient Israel and opened it up to the whole world.

**610. The lists of disciples** differ slightly from one book to another. The Gospel of Matthew lists Simon, Andrew (Simon's brother), James and John (the Sons of Zebedee), Philip, Bartholomew, Thomas, Matthew the tax collector, James the son of Alphaeus, Thaddaeus, Simon the Cananite, and Judas Iscariot. Luke refers to Simon as "the zealot" (a brand of political protestors) and mentions "Judas son of James" instead of Thaddaeus. Many of these men were pillars of the early church.

**611. Peter, who was called Simon** before Jesus renamed him, was the first leader of the early church. Peter had a long history with the Lord; he denied Christ three times before the cock crowed but went on in faith following Christ's death and resurrection to become exactly what his new name meant—"the rock."

**612. James and John,** both sons of Zebedee, were brothers. They both were active in the early church. Both had been especially close to Jesus, being present at the transfiguration. It is strongly believed that John went on to write the Gospel of John.

**613. Acts introduces the New Testament's** second most influential figure (Jesus was the first!), an educated, pious Jew and tentmaker named Saul. Born in what is now Turkey, Saul went to Jerusalem to learn from the esteemed rabbi Gamaliel, grandson of the legendary rabbi Hillel, the most prominent pharisaic rabbi of the first century. Given authority by the high priest to arrest followers of Christ in Damascus for blasphemy, Saul vigorously persecuted early Christians. His name was changed to Paul after he experienced a transforming vision and conversion.

**614. Paul** developed a strategy for his traveling ministry that he followed through all his journeys. He generally moved farther westward from Israel with each mission. When he entered a city for the first time, he would look for a synagogue or other place where he could find the Jews of the city. In the first century A.D., Jews were dispersed throughout the world. Hardly a city didn't have Jews who met together regularly. Sometimes synagogues were receptive to his message; at other times hearers were extremely hostile.

**615. When Paul was arrested** in Jerusalem for his "heretical" views, he demanded a trial in Rome before the emperor, his right as a Roman citizen—the equivalent of an American traveler demanding a hearing with the U.S. president.

**616. Many other missionaries** preached the gospel in the early years of the church. Their mission was to spread the Word to all parts of the known earth, as they had been commissioned to do by Jesus before he returned to heaven. Thanks to their efforts, Christianity gained a foothold quickly in nearly every part of the known world.

**617. Barnabas** was one of the earliest converts to Christianity and a close friend of Paul's. A Greek-speaking Jew from Cyprus, Barnabas's real name was Joseph, but because he was an excellent teacher, his friends called him Barnabas, which means "Son of encouragement." He accompanied Paul on the first missionary journey through Asia Minor.

**618. Timothy** was one of Paul's main helpers. Paul mentored the younger man through two letters (1 and 2 Timothy) and called him his "true son in the faith." Timothy also traveled on his own.

**619. Philip became a missionary and was the first** to preach the gospel to those living in Samaria. He is especially remembered for how he helped an Ethiopian read a passage from Isaiah. An angel directed him to go to the Ethiopian. Upon arriving they read the passage together. The foreigner asked to be baptized and became the first Ethiopian Christian.

**620. Silas** traveled as a missionary with Paul and Peter. He sang hymns joyously to Christ when he was imprisoned with Paul during the earthquake in Philippi. The jailer became a Christian because he was so moved by their display of faith. He was to Paul a "faithful brother."

**621. Phoebe is one of the few women** missionary figures of the New Testament. History indicates that it was not uncommon for women to be in leadership roles in the early church, though it was certainly not typical in Jewish synagogues. Phoebe traveled to Rome, most likely to bring Paul's letter (what we know as the Book of Romans) to the Christians there.

**622. Apollos** was a Jew from Alexandria. He was actually a missionary before he met Paul. John the Baptist had mentored him and helped Apollos become a powerful preacher. He found help for his questions about Jesus in Corinth when he spoke with Priscilla and Aquilla.

**623. Roman subjects incorporated** emperor worship into the local religion throughout the empire. In the provinces, leading citizens became priests in the imperial cult to cement their ties with Rome. (Augustus, however, exempted the Jews from the imperial cult.) Emperor worship continued as the official pagan religion of the empire until Christianity was recognized under the Emperor Constantine (A.D. 305–337).

**624. Paul stayed** longer in some cities than others. Some larger cities, such as Ephesus, became teaching centers through which he could reach outlying areas of the surrounding regions. Paul's goal was to teach his followers well enough so they could teach others. Those who were able to accept this role were called elders, overseers, and pastors. The focus, however, was not on building an organization, but on preaching the Word.

**625. The excellent highway system** constructed throughout the Mediterranean world by the Romans was traveled frequently by Paul. Built so Roman armies could move swiftly and their traders could deliver goods efficiently, the Roman roads also contributed to the spread of the Christian message.

**626. Since many Jews traveled to Jerusalem for annual feasts,** and since many apostles were on the road with Christ's message, Paul sometimes found that the gospel message had reached a town before he did. This was the case with Rome, the center of the world in its day. There were many disciples in this metropolis long before Paul reached it.

**627. The gospel of Christ** spread primarily by word of mouth. Sometimes the apostles would move on to another city only to receive a request for more teaching from the city they had recently left. So they would write letters to be read aloud to groups of individuals who met for teaching and encouragement. They also wrote letters while confined in prison.

**628. The *agrapha*** is a phrase meaning "things not written." It was used in the early church to refer to sayings of Jesus that his followers remembered, but which were not written down in any of the Gospels. For example, in Acts 20:35, Paul quotes the Lord Jesus as saying, "It is more blessed to give than to receive." Those words can't be found in any of the Gospels, so apparently that is one of the things the Lord's followers remembered him saying, and would cite him as the source, even though it was never written down as such.

**629. How do you tell the world** the "Good News" if you don't speak their language? The disciples were gathered in an upper room when all of a sudden "tongues of fire" touched the followers. They began to speak in other languages. Some people who saw them thought they were drunk. This was the arrival of the Holy Spirit that Jesus had promised. The disciples could now go and spread the Word of God everywhere.

**630. The early church** grew as a "communistic" society in which everyone shared, according to the reports in Acts. There was a utopian state of harmony depicted in these first days of the Christian community, although they were not yet called "Christians." A young man named Matthias was elected to replace Judas as one of the Twelve. The group prospered, made collective decisions, and enjoyed common ownership of goods, making the early Christians in Jerusalem a practical model for the kibbutz.

**631. In Acts 6, we see that seven young men were appointed** to see to the needs of the church people, in order to free up the time of the disciples and eventual apostles. Stephen, a gifted speaker, was one of these men. He was a skilled debater and angered many who could not argue well with him or win him over. Eventually these men became so angry that Stephen was arrested and tried before the Sanhedrin.

**632. The first martyr of the church was Stephen.** A young Pharisee named Saul was present. Eventually Saul would be converted and receive the name Paul. His conversion is a sign of the wondrous grace God has in store for those who believe in him. When Stephen was stoned, he died with a vision of Jesus in sight. He was at peace and thus incensed his captors even more. Before he died Stephen said, "Lord, do not hold this sin against them."

**633. The early church was not a perfect organization.** Early Christians were as sinful then as they can be now. One of the earliest instances of this appears in Acts 5. Ananias and his wife, Sapphira, lied about the amount of compensation they received after selling a field. Had they not pretended to sell it for less, it wouldn't have mattered, but since they did lie in order to keep back money for themselves, God took them both. As Peter told them, "You have lied to the Holy Spirit."

**634. Another famous Ananias** was Ananias of Damascus. When Paul was converted, he became blind. Ananias was told to go to the house where Paul was staying. He did so, though he knew that the man Saul was coming to arrest Christians. He prayed and the newly converted Paul received his sight back.

**635. Dorcas,** who was also called Tabitha, also received a miracle during the early days of the church. She lived in Joppa. She fell ill and then died. Her distressed friends sent for Peter, the "rock" of the church. He prayed for her even as she was dead! She was given her life back and sat up. Many of her friends became believers as a result of this miracle.

**636. Cornelius** was actually a Roman soldier and was stationed at Caesarea. He was a Gentile who had joined a synagogue in order to seek God. He was a "God fearer." An angel appeared to him one day and told Cornelius to send for Peter. When Peter came, Cornelius and his entire family learned about Jesus. They were baptized immediately and praised God.

**637. Eutychus** had been named well. His name means "lucky." While he was listening to Paul preach, he fell out of a third-story window (he fell asleep) and was lying still and believed to be dead when they reached him. Paul embraced him and he was healed. He had been blessed, not lucky, but his name seems appropriate!

**638. Philemon** had an interesting conversion experience. He was a wealthy Christian from Colosse, and he was converted by his slave, Onesimus. Onesimus had run away and eventually met the apostle Paul and became a believer. Paul sent him back to his master, Philemon, and urged Philemon to receive him as a "beloved brother." Philemon did so and was also saved!

**639. Lydia** is one of the few women mentioned in the early church. She was a seller of purple cloth and a Gentile, but sought God by going to a Jewish prayer center. She then met Paul and his fellow missionaries. She became converted, and eventually she and her family and even their workers were baptized. Paul and his friends stayed in her home.

**640. Stephanas** and his entire household were the first Christians to convert during Paul's ministry in Achaia. As the church grew in that area, Stephanas took a more active role in caring for other

new Christians. Paul was fond of him and his family and he especially enjoyed Stephanas's visit with him in Ephesus.

**641. Aquila and Priscilla** were a tent-making couple from Corinth.
They became Christians after listening to Paul preach. They were
dear friends of Paul and supported him to the very end, even risk-
ing their lives for him. They were loved and known in many
churches in Greece and Asia Minor.

**642. Acts closes with Paul incarcerated** and under a mild form
of house arrest in the imperial capital. He continued preaching the
gospel and writing letters to the churches he had established. Acts
says nothing more about Paul's appeal or ultimate fate, or that of
Peter. Both eventually disappear from the biblical account without any specific word about what happened to them. According to
well-established tradition, both apostles were martyred during
Emperor Nero's persecution of Christians after the great fire in
Rome in A.D. 64.

Part III

# Bible Times and *Trivia*

# 21

# The Bible Lands

**643. The Bible lands ceased to be the focal point for the ancient world** in the five centuries between the rebuilding of the temple at Jerusalem and the birth of Jesus. New empires rose, this time in Europe. First the Greeks and then the Romans overran the Bible lands. The Near Eastern peoples watched their land become ravaged of trees and precious metals to supply their conquerors. What forests had survived were cut down. The wilderness gave way to fields, and wild beasts were largely replaced by domesticated animals.

**644. Most rivers in the Bible lands** dry up during the rainless summer, but not the Nile. Heavy rains and melting snow feed the tributaries that form the Nile River. The torrent of water reaches Egypt during the late summer and it overflows the banks, leaving a fresh layer of fertile moist soil along its banks.

**645. The Holy Land is so small** that a soaring eagle can see almost all of it at once on a clear day. From Dan to Beersheba is little more than 150 miles, roughly the same distance as from New York City to Albany. From east to west, the Holy Land is even narrower. At its widest point, a hundred miles lie between the Mediterranean coast and the Arabian Desert on the east. The land in which such great events took place is only a little larger than the state of New Jersey and smaller than Belgium.

**646. This land that gave birth to our civilization** is inconspicuous on a map of the world. But no other part of the world, square foot for square foot, has played such a historic role in human history.

**647. The Holy Land's position at the crossroads** of three continents makes it a meeting ground for species of plants and animals of different origins. Almost every kind of bird, for example, that inhabits northern Africa, southern Europe, and western Asia has been seen at one time or another in the Bible lands. The fauna comes from as far away as Central Asia (the horse), equatorial Africa (the crocodile), and western Europe (the stork).

**648. The great variety of deserts, mountains, forests, grasslands, lakes, and seashores** provides nearly every possible habitat in which plants and animals can find the exact living conditions they need. About 2,250 species of trees and shrubs and annual and perennial plants grow in the Holy Land; Egypt, although much larger, has only fifteen hundred. About seven hundred species of mammals, birds, and reptiles are found in the Holy Land.

**649. The contrasts in the landscape are remarkable.** Mount Hermon rises to 9,400 feet, and its summit is arctic in climate. A little over a hundred miles away, at the Dead Sea, the climate is tropical. In the same glance you can see snow-capped mountains and sun-baked deserts. Alongside cultivated fields are stark deserts that afford scarcely enough pasture for flocks.

**650. The road from Jerusalem to Jericho** drops three thousand feet in only fifteen miles, and while fruit is growing on the farms around Jericho, it may be snowing in Jerusalem. The varied animals and plants, the many different landscapes, the abrupt changes in climate—all these realities were observed by the Bible's writers. And they put them to use to illustrate spiritual teachings.

**651. The Jordan Valley** is part of the Great Rift that extends from Turkey deep into Africa for four thousand miles. The Great Rift is the deepest chasm on the face of the globe. Unlike the Grand Canyon, which was formed by the process of erosion, great swells and cracking of the earth's crust caused huge blocks of land to collapse, leaving deep valleys that were flooded. In the Holy Land this formed the Jordan River, Lake Huleh, the Sea of Galilee, and the Dead Sea.

**652. The Jordan River** is among the most rapid of any rivers in the world. In approximately two hundred winding miles, it drops from almost two thousand feet *above* sea level to the surface of the Dead Sea, which is nearly thirteen hundred feet *below* sea level.

**653. The shore of the Dead Sea** is the lowest place on the land surface of the earth. This sea is also the saltiest body of water in the world, and nine times saltier than the oceans! It is so salty that it is impossible for a human swimmer to sink in it. During the Roman siege of Jerusalem in A.D. 70, a Roman commander sentenced some prisoners to death by having them thrown into the Dead Sea. The condemned men were thrown in from a hill, but they did not drown. Several times they were pulled out and tossed in again, yet each time they bobbed to the surface. The commander was impressed by this seeming miracle, since he did not understand its cause, and he pardoned the prisoners.

**654. Ancient Hebrews had an unlimited supply of salt.** They formed brine pits called "salt-pans" along the Dead Sea's flat coastal area. The sun evaporated the water in the pits, leaving behind an abundant supply of mineral salts.

**655. Salt was the chief economic product** of the ancient world, and the Hebrews used it in a variety of ways: for flavoring foods, preserving fish, curing meat, and pickling olives and vegetables. Infants were rubbed in salt to insure good health before swaddling. Salt was also believed to have been an antidote for tooth decay. Salt was an ingredient in the sacred anointing oil and ritual sacrifices symbolizing God's perpetual covenant with Israel (Num. 18:19).

**656. Cool streams, luxuriant pastures, and mountains shaggy with trees** are often described in the Bible. Yet visitors today usually see a bleak and barren landscape with waterless flatlands and bare hills. Almost everywhere the rocky bones of the earth show through the soil. An ancient Hebrew legend states that God had two bags of rocks when he made the world. He scattered the contents of one bag over the entire earth—but all the other rocks in the other bag he dropped on the small area of the Holy Land.

**657. The face of the land looked very different** than it does today. The first step toward agriculture was the cutting down of the forests. That is what Joshua told the tribes of Ephraim and Manasseh to do when they complained about the lack of farmland in the areas assigned to them: "But the forested hill country [shall be yours] as well. Clear it, and its farthest limits will be yours" (Josh. 17:18).

**658. Mount Sinai,** a solid block of reddish granite that rises steeply out of the desert, is only about three thousand feet high, not much in comparison to other mountains. It looms so dramatically out of the surrounding land, however, that the Israelites must have found it a fitting place for God to dwell.

**659. Mari, dating back to the eighteenth century B.C.,** was unveiled as one of the great cities of the ancient world. A ziggurat was unearthed, and so were twenty thousand clay tablets of writing. Among other things, these clay tablets preserve ancient police records that refer constantly to threats of Semitic nomads who lived on the frontiers of the kingdom and raided the towns of Mari.

**660. Haran, a little mud-brick settlement,** is one of the most important cities in the Near East. It was a key city connected by ancient trade routes to Ur. Nearly four thousand years ago, Abraham, his wife, Sarah, and his household set off with their herds and flocks on a historic journey to a Promised Land. Abraham's travels correspond to known migratory and commercial routes before Ur was conquered and abandoned in 1740 B.C.

**661. The city of Corinth** was one of the most important cities in the Roman Empire during Paul's lifetime. A commercial bridge between East and West, it attracted merchants, traders, and visitors from all around the Mediterranean area, making it something like the "Times Square" of its day.

**662. Solomon's ships sailed with metal and other items** of trade from Eziongeber on the Gulf of Aqaba to a place known as "Ophir." Its location has been heavily disputed and it was even believed to be a legendary land until a discovery was made near the ancient port of Joppa (Jaffa) in Israel of a Phoenician storage jar inscribed with the words "gold of Ophir."

**663. Ophir** very well may have been located in India or Ceylon, because the Bible states that the round-trip voyage took three years and that the ships brought back "gold, and silver, ivory, and apes, and peacocks" (1 Kings 10:22 KJV).

**664. The ancient cities of the Near East were usually walled,** and at night the gates were closed for protection against invaders. In case any of the citizens were unable to return before nightfall, one small opening was left in the gate, an opening known as "the needle's eye." It was so low and so narrow that a camel laden with riches could never fit through. Only when the owner unloaded the camel and left the load outside the gate could the camel, with its head bent low, squeeze through.

**665. Jesus' teaching in Matthew 19** seized on the analogy of the camel making its way through "the needle's eye" and compared it to a rich man trying to leave the earth with riches to get into heaven. A rich man can enter the kingdom of heaven—but only if he first casts off his worldly goods and, like the camel squeezing through the needle's eye, bows his head in humility.

**666. The civilization of the Egyptians** was already an ancient one by the time Joseph arrived there some 3,650 years ago. The first pyramid was built about five thousand years ago. It is known as the Step Pyramid because it rises in a series of steps or terraces to a height of 250 feet, much like the ziggurats of Babylon.

**667. The Great Pyramid of Cheops at Giza,** built only a few hundred years after the Step Pyramid, was the tallest structure ever erected until the nineteenth century. It rises to a height of 481 feet, and its base is 756 blocks of stone, many blocks weighing as much as five thousand pounds. This pyramid was built with no other mechanical equipment than the lever and the roller, because at that time the Egyptians had not yet learned the use of the wheel.

**668. More than thirty major pyramids** were built during the thousand years before Joseph. Each one guarded the body of a pharaoh entombed in a chamber deep inside the pile of stone blocks. However, no pyramids are mentioned in the Bible. Despite the fact that these structures would have certainly been the talk of the ancient world, the authors of the Bible didn't consider them worthy of note. They did not play a part in the unfolding of the biblical narrative.

# 22

# Festivals and Holidays

**669. Within the Hebrew calendar** there are twelve months of the year, just like our modern calendar. However, the Hebrew calendar starts in Tishri (September). The other months of the year are Heshvan, Kislev, Tevet, Shevat, Adar, Nisan, Iyar, Sivan, Tammuz, Av, and Elul.

**670. Rosh Hashanah** is the first day of the Hebrew year and is celebrated as we celebrate New Year's Day. Numbers 29:1 and Leviticus 23:24 explain the celebration in detail; typically the holiday falls in mid-September.

**671. Yom Kippur** is the Day of Atonement and comes on the tenth day of Tishri (Lev. 16:29; 23:27). The day falls toward the end of September.

**672. Succoth,** or the feast of Tabernacles or Booths, is celebrated the week of the fifteenth to the twenty-second of Tishri, concluding with a solemn assembly (Lev. 23:34–36).

**673. Solemn assembly** comes on the twenty-second day of Tishri (Lev. 23:36) and falls in our month of October.

**674. Dedication (Hanukkah)** is celebrated in the month of Kislev, on the twenty-fifth day (John 10:22).

**675. Purim** is celebrated in the month of Adar on the fourteenth and fifteenth days. The month falls between February and March. Purim commemorates the events of the Book of Esther (Esther 9:18–22). Therefore, it is not mentioned in Leviticus.

**676. Esther's triumph** is celebrated in the Jewish festival of Purim, a joyous festival to commemorate the Jews' deliverance from Haman while they lived under Persian rule. Since the time of the exile, Jews have observed this feast in recognition of God's continued deliverance of his people. As the Book of Esther is being read, each time the name of Haman is read, the listeners yell out, "Let his name be blotted out!" The names of Haman's sons are all read in one breath, to emphasize the fact that they were all hanged at the same time.

**677. The bitter herbs** for the celebration of the Passover mentioned in Numbers 9:11 may have included chicory, wild lettuce, and several plants whose leaves were gathered for use in salads; but they were most likely dandelions. Though we find them invading lawns in many parts of the world, the dandelion's original home was in the lands bordering the Mediterranean.

**678. Pesach,** or Passover, is celebrated on the fourteenth day of Nisan, which falls on our Palm Sunday, and can be in March or April depending on the year. Exodus 12 and Leviticus 23 explain the commemorative reasons in more detail.

**679. The Feast of Unleavened Bread** comes between the fifteenth and twenty-first days of the month of Nisan. This commemorates the Israelites' time in the desert and the food they were to eat—unleavened bread (Lev. 23:6).

**680. The Waving of the Sheaf of Firstfruits** celebrates the first-fruits of harvest (Lev. 23:10) and falls on the seventeenth day of Nisan, somewhere between March and April of our calendar year. It is just two days past the celebration called the Passover.

**681. Shavuoth,** or Pentecost, is held in the month of Sivan, on the sixth day. It is also known as the Feast of Weeks (Lev. 23:15).

# 23

# Family Life

## THE HUSBAND AND WIFE

**682. In the East, every company of travelers,** every tribe, every community, every family must have "a father," who is head of the group. Jabal "was the father of all such as handle the harp and organ." Jabal was the "father of such as dwell in tents and . . . have cattle" (Gen. 4:20–21 KJV). Easterners would not conceive of any band or group without somebody being "the father" of it.

**683. Under the patriarchal system,** the father is supreme in command. The authority of the father extends to his wife, his children, his children's children, his servants, and all his household. Many of the bedouin Arabs of today are under no government other than this patriarchal rule. When Abraham, Isaac, and Jacob lived in tents in the Land of Promise, they were ruled by this same system.

**684. Reverence of the children for their parents** and especially the father is almost universal in the Bible lands. It is quite customary for a child to greet the father in the morning by kissing his hand and standing before him in an attitude of humility, ready to receive any order, or waiting for permission to leave. After this the child is often pulled up onto the lap of the father.

**685. Women were confined to different roles than men.** They never ate with the men, and the husband and brothers were served first. While walking, women followed at a respectful distance. The woman was closely confined and watched with jealousy; and when she went out she was veiled from head to foot.

**686. The ancient Hebrew women did not have unrestrained freedom,** but they did have power in their role and influences within the family. A woman had tremendous influence for good or ill over her husband, and in most cases he showed her great respect. Sarah was treated like a queen by Abraham, and in matters of the household, she ruled in many ways.

**687. The tribute to the wife and mother in the Book of Proverbs indicates she was a person of great influence**: "Her husband has full confidence in her and lacks nothing of value" (31:11). "She speaks with wisdom, and faithful instruction is on her tongue" (31:26). "Her children arise and call her blessed; her husband also, and he praises her" (31:28).

**688. Several cities** mentioned in the Old Testament were built above underground springs. Megiddo and Hazor were two of these cities. In Hazor a woman would walk through the streets to a deep shaft. Then she descended thirty feet on five flights of stairs to the water tunnel, along which she proceeded to the water level to fill her large water jug. She needed considerable strength to climb back out of the watershaft with a heavy water jug. Gathering water was also a time for the women to socialize.

**689. The hum of the handmill grinding grain** would be one of the first sounds heard in the early morning of an Israelite village. For those who live in the Holy Lands, this sound is associated with home, comfort, and plenty. This task belonged to the women and began in the early morning because it would often take half the day to finish. When Jeremiah foretold judgment upon Israel for her sins, he said that God would "banish from them the sounds of joy and gladness, the voices of bride and bridegroom, *the sound of millstones* and the light of the lamp" (Jer. 25:10, emphasis added).

**690. Making clothes for the family** from the wool of their flocks was one of the responsibilities of Jewish women. Another task was the washing of clothing. The ancient women of Israel washed their clothes by going to nearby sources of water such as streams, pools, or watering troughs. Like Arab women, they dipped the clothes in and out of the water and then placed them on flat stones to beat them with a club. They carried the water in goatskins and had a vessel for rinsing.

**691. Collecting water from a well or spring** is another household task of the women. The same practice is used today in many places in the East just as it was done in Genesis: "it was toward evening, the time the women go out to draw water" (24:11). It is customary for Syrian women to carry the pitcher of water on their shoulders, although sometimes it is carried on their hip. Most Arabs of Palestine carry it on their heads. Scripture says that Rebekah carried her pitcher on her shoulder (Gen. 24:15).

**692. "A man carrying a jar of water . . ."** Carrying water was universally done by women. So when Jesus instructed two of his disciples, "Go into the city, and a man carrying a jar of water will meet you. Follow him" (Mark 14:13), it was an easy way of identifying the man. However when larger supplies of water were needed, men used large skins of sheep or goats for carrying it.

**693. The hard leather portable bucket with a rope** is brought to the well in addition to the pitcher in order to let down the bucket to the level of the water. The Samaritan woman who Jesus met at Jacob's well had brought all this with her, but Jesus did not have anything with him. This is why she said to him, "Sir, you have no bucket, and the well is deep" (John 4:11 NRSV).

## BEARING CHILDREN

**694. Levirate marriage.** The Israelites believed that it was very important for a man to have an heir. To preserve the property inheritance that God had given them, they had to convey it through family lines (Exod. 15:17–18). If a woman's husband died before she had borne an heir, the practice of levirate marriage (which was part of the Law of Moses) began. According to the law, when a woman was widowed, her dead husband's brother would marry her and the children of this marriage became heirs to the deceased brother. If a man refused to marry his widowed sister-in-law, he was publicly disgraced (Deut. 25:7–10).

**695. Many Israelite couples were unable to bear children.** Today we know that couples may be childless due to either the husband's or wife's sterility, but in Bible times only the wife was blamed for the problem. Barrenness was more than a physical or social problem. Deep religious meanings were attached to the problem as well. Moses promised the people that if they obeyed the Lord, blessing would follow: "Thou shalt be blessed above all people: there shall not be male or female barren among you, or among your cattle" (Deut. 7:14 KJV). So barrenness was believed to be a result of disobeying God.

**696. A barren couple spent a good deal of time examining** their past failures to see if any sin had been unconfessed. Childlessness became the main theme of the couple's prayers. Isaac begged the Lord to let his wife bear a child (Gen. 25:21). Hannah sobbed before the Lord and promised that if God would give her a son, she would dedicate him to the Lord's service (1 Sam. 1:11). When sin was ruled out as the cause of the problem, the wife would then inquire about different kinds of remedies.

**697. Modern excavations in Israel have produced many clay fertility figures.** These were supposed to help a woman get pregnant by "sympathetic magic." Each figurine was molded to look like a pregnant woman. As the barren woman handled it and kept it near her, she hoped to take on the likeness of the pregnant figure. Women also wore amulets, an ornament or gem worn against the body, to insure fertility.

**698. Adoption practices were common in ancient times.** Adoption solved many problems. The adopted son would care for the couple in their old age, provide them a proper burial, and inherit the family property. However, if the couple had a natural son after one had been adopted, he would become the rightful heir. After Bilhah's baby was born, it was placed in Rachel's lap. This act was a central part of the adoption ceremony. Other biblical adoptions include Moses adopted by Pharaoh's daughter and Esther adopted by Mordecai.

**699. Another ancient custom that continues in the East is the care for an infant child.** Instead of allowing the baby the free use of his arms and legs, it is bound hand and foot by swaddling bands, quite like a mummy. At birth the child is washed and rubbed with salt, and with its legs together and its arms at its side, it is wound around tightly with linen or cotton strips, four to five inches wide and five or six yards long. The band is also placed under the chin and over the forehead. Not only does the Bible describe the baby Jesus as swaddled, but Ezekiel also mentions the custom of swaddling (Ezek. 16:4).

**700. It was considered a privilege and a duty for the Jewish mother to breastfeed her infant.** But sometimes a mother was not physically able to do so. For these women, a wet nurse was secured. This wet nurse (usually unrelated to the baby) fed the baby her own breast milk. When Pharaoh's daughter found Moses floating among the reeds of the Nile, one of her first orders was to get a Hebrew woman who could nurse him.

**701. The weaning of a child is an important event in the domestic life of the East.** In many places it is celebrated by a festive gathering of friends, by feasting, religious ceremonies, and sometimes the formal presentation of rice to the child. Hebrew babies are often nursed for two years and sometimes for four or five. It was probably after age three that Hannah weaned Samuel and brought him to be presented to the Lord. A scriptural example of the weaning feast is found in Gen. 21:8, when Isaac was weaned and dedicated to the Lord.

**702. Names were very important in the world of the Old Testament.** Hebrew names usually carried meaning about the person's character, praise to God, or the location or circumstances surrounding the child's birth. Jewish people believed that they must first know a person's name before they could know the person. The name *Jesus* is a Greek form of the Hebrew name *Joshua,* which means "salvation of Yahweh." The name was given by one or both parents. Scripture indicates that the mother usually named the infant.

**703. Many cultures in the world today practice circumcision for hygienic reasons.** Some primitive tribes perform the operation on infants and young boys, while others wait until the boys reach puberty or are ready for marriage. These traditions have remained unchanged for centuries. For the Israelites, circumcision signified that the infant was being taken into the covenant community. This ritual remains a hallmark of Judaism today. Flint knives were used until New Testament times when they were finally replaced by metal. Jewish boys were circumcised on the eighth day.

**704. Recent studies have confirmed** that the safest time to perform circumcision is on the eighth day of life. Vitamin K, which causes blood to coagulate, is not produced in sufficient amounts until the fifth to seventh day. On the eighth day the body contains 10 percent more prothrombin than normal; prothrombin is also important in the clotting of blood.

**705. Since all firstborns were God's possession,** it was necessary for the Israelite family to redeem, or buy back, the firstborn infant from God. The redemption price was five shekels of silver, given to the priests when the child was one month old—possibly an amount of time to be certain the child would live (Num. 18:15–16). Scripture doesn't tell us about the redemption ceremony itself.

**706. By rabbinic times the redemption ceremony** took place in the child's home with a priest and other guests present. The rite began when the father presented the child to the priest. The priest would then ask the father, "Do you wish to redeem the child or do you want to leave him with me?" The father answered that he would redeem the child and handed the priest five silver coins. The priest would then declare, "Your son is redeemed!" After the priest pronounced a blessing on the child, he joined the invited guests at a banquet table.

# 24

# Manners and Customs

**707. Knowing the manners and customs of the East** (those living in countries east of Europe) is necessary for a thorough understanding of the Bible. Westerners can easily misunderstand the motives and meanings of why our ancient Israelite forefathers and mothers did and said what they did in the Scriptures.

## Clothing and Accessories

**708. The manner of dress in the Eastern countries** is largely the same as it was centuries ago. There is a prevalent view in the Bible lands that it is morally wrong to change anything that is ancient.

**709. The inner garment.** The tunic was a shirt worn next to the skin. It was made of leather, haircloth, wool, linen, or in modern times, usually cotton. The simplest style was without sleeves and reached to the knees or ankles. The well-to-do wore it with sleeves and it extended to the ankles. Both men and women wore this garment, although there was no doubt a difference in style and pattern in what was worn. The garment of Jesus for which the Roman soldiers cast lots was a tunic without seams.

**710. The garment Jacob gave to Joseph** (Gen. 37:3), translated in the Septuagint and Vulgate Bible as the "coat of many colors," is the same expression used for the garment worn by Tamar, the daughter of King David. It is translated in Greek and Latin as "a sleeved tunic" (2 Sam. 13:18). For this reason, many Bible scholars believe it was a long undergarment with sleeves. The working classes usually wore a short tunic, whereas the aristocracy wore a long tunic with sleeves.

**711. The girdle.** If the tunic was ungirded (or untied) it would interfere with a person's ability to walk freely, and so a girdle was always worn when leaving home (2 Kings 4:29; Acts 12:8). There were and still are two types. A common variety is made of leather, usually six inches wide, with clasps. This was the kind worn by Elijah (2 Kings 1:8), and by John the Baptist (Matt. 3:4). The other, a more valuable type, is made of linen or sometimes silk or embroidered material. The girdle served as a pouch to carry money and other things, as well as to fasten a man's sword to his body.

**712. The outer garment or "mantle."** The outer garment that a Palestinian villager wears is a large cloak that serves as an overcoat. It is made of wool or goat's hair and serves as a shelter from the wind and rain, as well as a blanket at night. It was this outer garment or mantle with which Elijah smote the waters of the Jordan and crossed over. When Elijah was taken up to heaven this mantle was thrown down to Elisha (2 Kings 2:8–13).

**713. Because the outer garment was a man's covering by night,** the law did not allow anybody to take this as pledge or security on a loan because it would deprive him of his means of keeping warm while sleeping. When a garment was taken, it had to be returned by sunset (Exod. 22:26–27).

**714. Hair.** The Jews of the Bible gave much attention to the care of their hair. The young people loved to wear it long and curled (Song of Sol. 5:11), and they were proud to have thick hair (2 Sam. 14:25–26). Middle-aged men and priests would occasionally cut their hair, but not very often.

**715. Baldness was scarce,** and suspicion of leprosy was often attached to the condition. When the youth said to Elisha, "Go on up, you baldhead!" (2 Kings 2:23), he was using an extreme curse.

**716. Baldness disqualified a man from the priesthood,** as is demonstrated by Leviticus 21:5. Priests were not allowed to shave their heads or rip their clothes, or even to mourn a mother's or father's death (Lev. 21:10–11).

**717. Men allowed their beards to grow long** and rarely if ever cut them.

**718. Jews always wore a turban** in public. At certain seasons of the year it is dangerous to expose the head to the rays of the sun. This turban was made of thick material that was wound several times around the head. Both Job and the prophet Isaiah mention the use of the turban as a headdress (Job 29:14).

**719. Wearing what is appropriate.** The Law of Moses forbade men to wear women's clothing or women to wear men's clothing (Deut. 22:5).

**720. The dress of women** was different in detail from men's clothing rather than in style. They too wore a tunic and cloak, but in every case their dress was a little more elaborate. The veil was the distinctive female apparel. All females, with the exception of maidservants, women of low status, and prostitutes, wore a veil.

**721. The headgear of Bethlehem women** shed light on biblical customs. The headgear included a high cap on the front of which might have been sewn rows of gold and silver coins. There was also a veil, perhaps six feet long and four feet wide that covered the cap but left the coins showing. Some had embroidery work and some were nearly covered with needlework.

**722. Jewish men did not wear jewelry** as a rule. They often carried a cane or staff with some ornamentation at the top. Certain men wore a ring on their right hand, or on a chain around their neck. This was the signet ring or seal and served as the personal signature of its owner.

**723. Jewish women did use ornaments,** such as in elaborate braiding of their hair (which Peter and Paul spoke against in 1 Peter and 1 Timothy). Earrings were worn by women of Jacob's family (Gen. 35:4), and the gold earrings of the Israelite women contributed to the gold in Aaron's golden calf (Exod. 32:2). Abraham's servant had two bracelets ready to give Rebekah, and in the third chapter of his prophecy, Isaiah lists many feminine ornaments (Isa. 3:18–20).

**724. Each society has its own standards of physical beauty.** It is difficult to know just what the ancient Hebrews found beautiful. Most of the attractive women mentioned in the Bible are not described in detail. The writer usually notes simply that a woman was "beautiful." Some of the most important women in the Old Testament were said to be beauties: Sarah, Rebekah, Rachel, Bathsheba, Tamar, Abishag, and Esther.

**725. What did Jesus wear?** He must have worn the turban, worn by both the rich and poor alike. Under his turban his hair would be rather long and his beard uncut. His tunic, the undergarment, was one piece without a seam. It was therefore of some value and had probably been given to him by one of the wealthier women who ministered to him. Over this he wore the mantle, loose and flowing. This cloak probably was not white, because we're told it turned white during the transfiguration. It was most likely a common blue or it may have been white with brown stripes. Jesus did have at the four corners of this mantle the tsitsith (fringe).

**726. In Old Testament times practically all clothing** was made from sheep's wool. We are accustomed to seeing sheep that have been bred for their white wool, but in biblical times most sheep had brown coats or were black and white.

**727. The hair clipped from goats** was woven into coarse cloth to make the black tents in which the nomads lived. The size of the tent depended on the wealth of the owner, but even the simplest tent was divided by curtains into a front room for entertaining and another room for cooking and housing the children.

## TENTS

**728. Tents** are one of the earliest family shelters mentioned in the Bible. The first reference to tent life in the Scriptures is found in Genesis 4:20, when Jabal is described as "the father of such as dwell in tents." Following the flood Japheth was said to have lived "in the tents of Shem" (Gen. 9:27 KJV). The patriarchs, Abraham, Isaac, and Jacob, lived most of their lives in tents, in and around the land of Canaan. The children of Israel lived in tents during their forty years in the wilderness and for many years after entering the Promised Land. Hundreds of years later, in the days of David, it was said to the king, "The ark, and Israel, and Judah, abide in tents" (2 Sam. 11:11).

**729. The bedouin's home** is his tent, which is made of black goat hair. This is the same material as the sackcloth of Bible times. The main overhead portion is a large awning that is held up by poles. The ends of the tent are drawn out by cords tied to pegs and driven into the ground. It was one of these tent pegs that Jael used to drive into Sisera's head while he slept (Judg. 4:21).

**730. The tent is usually oblong** and divided into two and sometimes three rooms by goat-hair curtains. The entrance leads into the men's quarters where guests are received. Beyond this is the area for the women and children. Sometimes a third section is used for servants or cattle. The women in the inner section are screened from the view of those in the reception room, but they can hear what goes on. Remember Sarah overheard the angel and laughed (Gen. 18:10–15).

**731. Bible time nomads** were constantly on the move so their furnishings included only the necessities. Rugs covered the ground and bedding was brought out at night. They laid on mats or carpets and covered themselves with their outer garments worn during the day. In a nomad tent you would find bags of grain and a handmill and mortar with which to pound the grain. Hanging from the poles would be skin bags or bottles for water and other liquids; a leather bucket to draw water up from any well available; an earthen pitcher used by women to carry water; and a few pots, kettles, and pans. Serving dishes included mats, platters or larger dishes, and cups for drinking. For some, a primitive lamp was used at night. If the family had a camel, then the camelbags or saddle would have been used as seats.

**732. Seeing new tents** is and was out of the ordinary. Even today goat clippings are accumulated over the course of the year, and with these, the women make new strips to repair the old tent. The section that is most worn is ripped out and a new piece is sewn in. The old piece is then used for a side curtain. Each year new strips of cloth replace the old ones and the "house of hair" is handed down from father to son without it being completely old or new at any one time.

**733. As the tent-dweller's family grows larger** or he becomes richer, he adds on another section to his old tent. Isaiah had this process in mind when he compared the prophetic prosperity of Israel to a bedouin tent.

> Enlarge the place of your tent,
>> stretch your tent curtains wide,
>> do not hold back;
> lengthen your cords,
>> strengthen your stakes.
>
> Isaiah 54:2

## HOUSES

**734. A life of agriculture** took the place of the wandering life of nomads after Israel had been in the land of Canaan for many years and settled in. Houses began to take the place of tents. The average home of the common people was a one-room shelter. In Bible times, people spent as much time as possible in God's outdoors. The Hebrew word for house is *bayith* and means shelter. It served only as a place to rest after a day outside. The sacred writers referred to God as a "shelter" or a "refuge" (Ps. 61:3; Isa. 4:6).

**735. The one-room houses** were usually made of clay bricks dried in the sun (similar to adobe houses in Mexico), but sometimes they were made of rough, local sandstone and set with a mud mortar.

Only the palaces or houses of the wealthy were constructed of hewn stones, like the palaces of Solomon (1 Kings 7:9).

**736. The roofs** of these humble houses were made by laying beams across from wall to wall, then putting down a mat of reeds or thorn bushes and over it a coating of clay or mud. Sand and pebbles were then scattered over this and a stone roller was used to make it smooth enough to shed rain.

**737. Earthy homes** create challenges unfamiliar to westerners. It is not uncommon to see grass growing on the tops of the houses, as the Bible even references, "May they be like grass on the roof, which withers before it can grow" (Ps. 129:6; see also 2 Kings 19:26; Isa. 37:27). With a dirt roof, leaks often soak through after a heavy rain. The Book of Proverbs compares this dripping to a quarrelsome wife (Prov. 19:13; 27:15). Not only did dripping cause trouble, but snakes often crawled in through cracks, and thieves could dig through and get into the house. Job said, "In the dark they dig through houses, which they had marked for themselves in the daytime" (Job 24:16 KJV).

**738. The houses with one room** were in the villages and those with more than one room were in the cities. If a house with two rooms was to be built, the rooms weren't placed side by side. Rather the breadth of another room was left between the two rooms, and a wall was constructed between the ends to make an open court. If there were three or more rooms, a room would be substituted for the wall at the end of the court and there would be more rooms around the courtyard, making a secluded area from the street.

**739. Cisterns** were often built in the courtyards for water, and fires were built for warmth, as described by Simon Peter's experience in the courtyard of the high priest's house where Jesus was being tried (John 18:18). The courtyard was a place to eat and also a place to bathe. When David looked down from his palace rooftop and saw the beautiful Bathsheba bathing (2 Sam. 11:2), she was in the courtyard of her house, a protected place not visible to ordinary observation.

**740. The roof of an Arab's house** was and is used today for a large variety of purposes, much like it was used in the days of the prophets and the apostles. It is used for storage (Josh. 2:6), as a place to sleep (1 Sam. 9:26), a spot for gathering in times of excitement to see down the streets (Isa. 22:1), a place of public proclamations (Matt. 10:27), a place of worship and prayer (Zeph. 1:5; Acts 10:9), and as a way of escape in time of danger (Matt. 24:17; Mark 13:15; Luke 17:31).

**741. Candles** weren't a part of Bible life. The King James Version of the Bible frequently uses the word *candle* because candles were so widely used at the time that version was written. However, a literal translation of the original words would use *lamp* or *light*. Bible characters knew nothing about candles.

**742. A lamp** was considered to be the Palestinian peasant's one luxury that was a necessity. When the sun set, the door of his house was shut, and then the lamp was lit. To sleep without a light was considered by most villages to be a sign of extreme poverty. When a late traveler saw a light in a house, he knew there was life there. To wish a man's light be put out was to wish on him a terrible curse.

**743. Fuel** is so scarce in the Holy Lands that peasants often burn dried dung and sell sticks that they gather. Dried grass and withered flowers are also carefully gathered into bundles and used for making a fire. This was done in the days of old as well. As Jesus said, "The grass of the field, which today is, and tomorrow is cast into the oven" (Matt. 6:30 KJV; Luke 12:28). Another popular fuel is thorns or thorny shrubs. The widow of Zarephath gathered sticks to build a fire (1 Kings 17:10), but the fire built in the courtyard of the high priest where Simon Peter warmed himself was built with charcoal (John 18:18 KJV).

## GUESTS AND HOSPITALITY

**744. A custom of sending double invitations** to a special event has been observed in some parts of the East. Several examples of this custom are found in the Bible. At some time before the feast is to be served, an invitation is sent forth; then when the appointed time draws near, a servant is sent again to announce that everything is now ready. One example of this is in the parable of the great supper: "A certain man was preparing a great banquet and invited many guests. At the time of the banquet he sent his servant to tell those who had been invited, 'Come, for everything is now ready'" (Luke 14:16–17).

**745. "Then the master told his servant,** 'Go out to the roads and country lanes and make them come in, so that my house will be full'" (Luke 14:23). In the East the one invited is expected to reject an invitation upon the first invite. He must be urged to accept. All the while he expects to attend, but he must allow the one inviting him the privilege of "compelling him" to accept.

**746. Ancient banquets** were usually held at night in brilliantly lighted rooms, and anybody who was excluded from the feast was said to be cast out of the lighted room into "the outer darkness" of the night. In the teaching of Jesus, the day of judgment is likened to being excluded from the banquet (Matt. 8:12). In the East a lamp is usually kept burning all night. Because of people's fear of the darkness, the Savior could have chosen no more appropriate words than "outer darkness" for the future punishment of the unrighteous.

**747. Seats** were uncommon in early Bible times, except in the king's circle or at other times of ceremony. The prophet Amos was the first of the biblical writers to refer to the custom of "stretch[ing] themselves upon their couches" when eating (Amos 6:4). By the time of Jesus the Romans were accustomed to reclining on couches at supper.

**748. A triclinium** was a common dining setup of the Romans. It included a short square table with three couches to surround three sides of the perimeter. The fourth side was left open so the servant could reach the table easily.

**749. Guests of honor** were held in special esteem when they were assigned to a room with a higher floor than the rest of the house. Many houses had such a room for special company.

**750. Guests were also honored** by being seated at the right of the host during meals. The next highest place was at the left of the host. Jesus condemned the Pharisees for their insistence on having the highest places of distinction when they were invited to a banquet.

**751. Dancing** was often part of the entertainment at feasts. When the prodigal son returned home, there was music and dancing (Luke 15:24–25). Mainly the women and girls danced, although sometimes men did, too, as David did when the ark was brought into Jerusalem (2 Sam. 6:14). But there is no scriptural record that Jewish men danced with the women.

**752. Sharing hospitality with others** was an integral part of Israelite life. Men of the East believed guests were sent by God. Therefore providing for their hospitality became a sacred duty. When Abraham entertained three strangers who proved to be angels, his enthusiasm seemed to indicate this same belief (Gen. 18:2–7). We typically think of guests as friends or business acquaintances. But in the East there are three types of guests: friends, strangers, and enemies.

**753. Strangers as guests.** An old Eastern proverb says, "Every stranger is an invited guest." Like Abraham, the bedouin Arab of today will sit in the entrance of his tent in order to be on the watch for a stranger and guest (Gen. 18:1). In the New Testament, when Paul taught the Roman believers to be "given to hospitality" (Rom. 12:13 KJV), he was referring to the same thing. The Greek word he used for hospitality is pronounced "fil-ox-en-ee-ah," which means "love to strangers."

**754. Enemies as guests.** One remarkable aspect of Eastern hospitality is that an enemy can be received as a guest. As long as he remains in that relationship, he is perfectly safe and is treated as a friend. Certain tribes of tent-dwellers live by the rule that an enemy who has "once dismounted and touched the rope of a single tent is safe."

**755. Customs of hospitality and honor for guests** are very important in the East. When a guest first enters a home, bowing between the guest and host will take place. An expressive custom is that of saluting with the head erect and the body inclined forward by raising the hand to the heart, mouth, and forehead. The symbolic meaning of this is to say, "My heart, my voice, and my brain are all at your service." On many occasions those who are used to this custom enter into a more complete bow afterward.

**756. The greetings** upon entering an Arab house or a bedouin tent go something like this: The host will say, "Salam alakum," which means "Peace be on you." The guest will then respond with the words "Wa alakum es-salam," meaning "And on you peace." The greeting is then followed with a kiss. The men will place their right hand on the other's left shoulder and kiss his right cheek, and then reverse the action. Scriptural examples of the kiss are found when Jacob kissed his father; Esau kissed Jacob; Joseph kissed his brothers; Aaron kissed Moses; Moses kissed Jethro; David and Jonathan kissed each other; and the father of the prodigal son kissed him when he returned home.

**757. Guests take off their shoes** before entering the main room of a house. This is necessary because they will sit on a mat, rug, or divan, with their feet beneath them. Shoes would soil the couch and their clothes. This led to the custom of removing shoes upon entering sacred places. At the burning bush the Lord told Moses, "Take off your sandals, for the place where you are standing is holy ground" (Exod. 3:5).

**758. The Eastern guest is offered water for washing his feet** after the bowing, greeting, and kissing are completed. A servant will assist the guest by pouring water over the guest's feet above a copper basin, rubbing them with his hands, and wiping them on a towel. When Jesus was with his disciples, he took the place of the servant and washed their feet.

**759. The custom of anointing guests** is an ancient one among nations of the East. Olive oil is often used by itself, but sometimes it is mixed with spices. Simon the Pharisee was accused of being inhospitable because he didn't anoint Jesus (Luke 7:46). David memorialized this custom when he wrote in his shepherd psalm, "You anoint my head with oil" (Ps. 23:5).

**760. Many accounts of anointing** are found in the Bible, each carrying different meanings of the custom as a way of showing courtesy, respect, and devotion; for healing purposes; and as a symbol of the pouring out of God's Spirit.

**761. One of the first beverages** a guest is offered is a drink of water. This is to recognize him as a person worthy of peaceful reception. To give a drink of water is the simplest way to pledge friendship with a person. The words of Jesus in the Gospel of Mark (9:41) demonstrate this custom, "Anyone who gives you a cup of water in my name because you belong to Christ will certainly not lose his reward."

**762. The sharing of food** in Eastern cultures is a very special act of hospitality. It is a way of making a covenant of peace and fidelity. When Abimelech wanted a permanent covenant with Isaac, the confirmation of that covenant came when Isaac "made a feast for them, and they ate and drank" (Gen. 26:30).

**763. "The guest while in the house is its lord."** This is a true statement of the spirit of Eastern hospitality. One of the first greetings a Palestinian host will give his guest is to say, "Hadtha beitak," meaning "This is your house." This phrase is repeated many times during the guest's stay. There was a similar attitude between Lot and his guests when he said, "My lords, please turn aside to your servant's house" (Gen. 19:2).

**764. Defending to the death.** In the lands of the East, when a host accepts a man as his guest he agrees to defend the guest from all possible enemies during the time of his stay, whatever the cost. The psalmist felt utterly secure, though he had enemies close to him, when he knew that God was his host. "You prepare a table before me in the presence of my enemies" (Ps. 23:5).

**765. Eastern people make mention of God in daily conversation.** An astonished person will exclaim, "Mashallah," or "See what God has done!" which is the exact expression used by Balaam centuries ago (Num. 23:23). If a person is asked if he expects to do a certain thing, he will answer, "If God wills." Such an answer was recommended by James in his epistle (James 4:15).

**766. The Eastern manner of speaking** often includes picturing what is meant with figurative language and exaggerated expressions or even by demonstrating a concept. If John the Baptist had spoken like a westerner, he might have said, "Your pretense of virtue and good birth far exceed your actual practice of virtue." But being an easterner he said, "You brood of vipers! Who warned you to flee from the coming wrath? Produce fruit in keeping with repentance. And do not think you can say to yourselves, 'We have Abraham as our father.' I tell you that out of these stones God can raise up children for Abraham" (Matt. 3:7–9).

## WORSHIP

**767. Canaanites and Phoenicians worshiped many nature gods**. Baal, who was regarded as master of the earth, had an arm that hurled bolts of lightning, and his voice caused thunder. The Israelites referred to Baal as Baal-zebul or Beelzebub, which means "lord of the flies," no doubt referring to the hordes of flies that buzzed around the animals sacrificed to this god. By New Testament times Beelzebub had become a title for Satan.

**768. Mutual gods.** Just as the Israelites were attracted to Canaanite gods, so were the Philistines. Their deities—Dagon, Ashtaroth, and Baal-zebub—were all related to Canaanite gods.

**769. The father was the priest of the whole family** in the days of the early patriarchs. This honor and responsibility was then passed down to the firstborn son after the father's death. This practice continued until the Law of Moses transferred the right to the tribe of Levi, who became the priests of the Hebrew nation.

**770. The altar.** Throughout the Old Testament many altars were built and described. After Abraham pitched his tent in the vicinity of Bethel, the Scripture says, "There he built an altar to the LORD and called on the name of the LORD" (Gen. 12:8). Altars served as monuments of holiness and provided an approach to God through sacrifice.

**771. Clay figures called teraphim** were household gods that served as guardian angels of the home in Babylonia. At the death of a father they were passed down to the eldest son. When Jacob left the home of Laban in Haran, Rachel stole the teraphim that belonged to her father (Gen. 31:19). This made Laban very upset, so he pursued Jacob's caravan. Even though Jacob told his family to get rid of the foreign gods and purify themselves, the teraphim appeared several times in later history of the Israelites.

**772. Religious education** in the family became a special mark of Judaism. The Law of Moses was very specific in its requirements that parents must train their children in the knowledge of God and his laws. The emphasis on this education in the family has contributed largely to the permanence of the Jews in history.

**773. The pilgrimage made to the place of sanctuary** was a very important part of Hebrew life. "Three times a year all your men are to appear before the Sovereign LORD, the God of Israel" (Exod. 34:23). The whole family could go, but the men and boys were required to go. Remember Joseph and Mary traveled a day's journey on their return from Jerusalem before discovering that Jesus was missing. Because clans traveled together, parents could go for hours without seeing their sons.

**774. Jewish boys** had to be able to recite "the Shema," a prayer, by the age of twelve. The prayer was the quotation of three passages from the Pentateuch that was repeated morning and evening by Jewish men. The three passages were from Deuteronomy 6:4–9; 11:13–21; and Numbers 15:37–41.

**775. The idea of *minyan*** is central to the spiritual life of Jewish people. While anyone can pray at any time, before an official prayer service can be held there must be at least ten men present. This group of ten men is called a *minyan*. It was stated in the law that whenever ten adult men were gathered together in the name of God, the Lord himself would actually be present in the room with them. Any room then became consecrated ground, a holy place where men could perform their religious rituals and worship God.

**776. The early gathering place** for Christian worship was in people's homes. The earliest excavation of a church by archaeologists, where a date has been assigned (dating back to the third century A.D.), is of a room within a house that was set apart for worship and furnished as a chapel. In the days of the apostles, believers also took seriously their responsibility to care for believers who came to their town. In a time of persecution, this refuge was very important to those who traveled to spread the gospel.

## FOOD

**777. A single large olive tree** in biblical times provided an entire family with all of the oil it needed for food and lamps, as much as half a ton of it a year. The tree gave a year-round crop because both the unripe and the ripe fruit are edible. So the olive leaf in the dove's beak promised a rebirth of life to Noah and his family.

**778. The ordinary food** of the average Hebrew of Bible times was bread, olives, oil, buttermilk, and cheese from their flocks, fruits and vegetables from their orchards and gardens, and meat on rare occasions.

**779. The eating of raw grain** is a modern custom in Palestine that dates back to very ancient days. Contemporary Arabs often pick the heads of grain, rub them in their hands, and eat them. Some Pharisees approached Jesus and his disciples as they ate raw grain in the fields. "One Sabbath Jesus was going through the grainfields, and his disciples began to pick some heads of grain, rub them in their hands and eat the kernels" (Luke 6:1).

**780. When grain in the wheat field** has passed the "milk stage" and begun to harden, it is called "fereek" and is considered delicious eaten raw. For centuries the unwritten law of hospitality has been that wayfarers may eat some of the wheat as they pass by or through a field, but they must not carry any away with them. The law of God allowed this same privilege in Deuteronomy 23:35.

**781. Parched grain** is another common food eaten in Bible times. It is prepared with grains of wheat that are not fully ripe. They are roasted in a pan or on an iron plate. The grain is eaten either with or without bread. Jesse sent some of it with David to his older sons in the army (1 Sam. 17:17). Abigail included some in her gift to David (1 Sam. 25:18), and David received some from friends after he had fled from Absalom (2 Sam. 17:28).

**782. Besides wheat and barley,** millet and spelt ("rie" in some translations) were also grown. Wheat was the first choice of people, with barley reserved for the poor. Spelt is actually a weak strain of wheat.

**783. Bread** is unquestionably the principal food of the East and is considered sacred. In some places of Palestine, there is such a reverence for bread that people will not rise to greet a guest if they are in the midst of breaking bread together. The guest will have to wait until they are finished. Everything about bread, from the sowing of grain to the baking, is done in the name of God.

**784. The sacredness of the bread.** There is a universal Eastern custom of *breaking* bread and not cutting it. To cut bread would be thought of as cutting life itself. Because Christ broke bread when he instituted the ordinance of the Lord's Supper, the expression "breaking of bread" came to refer to the practice of taking communion.

**785. The expression "eating bread"** is often used in the Bible to mean eating a whole meal. When the Bible says, "The Egyptians might not eat bread with the Hebrews" (Gen. 43:32 KJV), it means that they would likely not eat a meal with them. In Lamentations 4:4 we read: "The young children ask bread, and no man breaketh it unto them" (KJV). The expression "breaking of bread" means the taking of a meal.

**786. The Israelite's Egyptian diet** included leeks, onion, and garlic, and the prophet Isaiah mentions a "garden of cucumber" (Isa. 1:8 KJV). Gourds were also used (2 Kings 4:39).

**787. The two most widely used vegetables** in Bible times, however, were beans and lentils. The most famous biblical use of lentils was, of course, the selling of Esau's birthright for a meal of lentil stew with bread (Gen. 25:34).

**788. Fruits** included olives and grapes, which were eaten fresh and also dried as raisins (1 Sam. 25:18) or made into wine. Pomegranates were grown for their juice, and it is possible, though not likely, that apples were grown as well. Both of the latter fruits are mentioned in Song of Songs.

**789. Figs,** though mentioned often enough and thought of largely as food by contemporary sources, were grown for medicinal purposes as well as general consumption in Bible times.

**790. Wine** was the most common alcoholic drink. It is mentioned throughout the Bible. The vineyard and the process of making wine are common examples in Jesus' teachings, most likely because they were familiar analogies for people since the beverage was so common.

**791. Beer** was brewed in Egypt and Mesopotamia, and perhaps the Israelites were familiar with this beverage also. Also brewed in these two areas was a wine made of figs.

**792. Milk** was considered a substantial food for all ages in Bible times. The Promised Land was often called "a land flowing with milk and honey" (Exod. 3:8; 13:5; Josh. 5:6; Jer.11:5). A form of milk that is commonly used among the Arabs today is called "leben," which means "white." It is like our sour milk curds. It was probably this that Abraham gave to his guests (Gen. 18:8) and also that Jael gave to Sisera (Judg. 4:19; 5:25).

**793. Butter and cheese** were made from the rich cream and curds (Prov. 30:33; Job 10:10). As the Hebrews didn't eat meat often, these would have served as a protein source for the people.

**794. Meat** was only eaten on special occasions, such as when a stranger or guest was entertained, or when a feast was made. Kings and wealthy men, on the other hand, ate meat often. The daily menu of four kinds of meat for King Solomon's court is given in Scripture: beef, mutton, game, and fowl (1 Kings 4:23).

**795. Nuts** also count as a protein source, and though meat was rare, nuts weren't. Almonds and pistachios are mentioned in Genesis 43:11.

**796. Numerous references to honey and honeycomb** in God's Word are proof that the Holy Land abounded with the sweet stuff. Many scriptural citations indicate that wild honey was very common, being found in cavities of trees, such as when Jonathan discovered and ate some honey (1 Sam. 14:25–27). It is also mentioned as being found in the holes of rock, where it was often extracted (Ps. 81:16), and even in the dried carcasses of animals, as when Samson ate honey from the carcass of the lion (Judg. 14:8–9).

**797. Honey is used** in the poetic books of the Hebrew Bible to make many comparisons. The judgments of God are compared to it (Ps. 19:10). Pleasant words are likened to it (Prov. 16:24), as are knowledge and wisdom to the soul (Prov. 24:13–14). And the bride and bridegroom of Solomon's Song speak of honey (Song of Sol. 4:11; 5:1).

**798. Seasoning** most often refers to salt (Job 6:6). However, other types of spice, such as dill ("anise" in the KJV), mint, cumin, and coriander are also mentioned.

**799. What is "kosher"?** Many people, Jew and Gentile alike, commonly ask if something is kosher, loosely using the term to mean "permissible" or "okay." *Kosher* is a Yiddish word for "proper" that derives from the Hebrew word *kashrut.* Although in the modern sense we commonly associate "kosher" with only dietary laws, the notion of what is "proper" covers a broad range of items that must be done in accordance with the law.

**800. Hand washing** was very important to the Israelites. They were careful to wash their hands before each meal. Water was poured (most often by a servant) over the hands to be washed as they were held over a basin. Because the Hebrew people did not eat with silverware, washing was a necessity. Elisha poured water over the hands of Elijah in 2 Kings 3:11. As Elijah's servant, this was an important part of Elisha's duties.

**801. Meals were eaten** on a mat spread on the ground (like a picnic blanket), or at a low table when the diners were commoners. The Hebrew word pronounced "Shool-khawn," usually translated "table," has as its root meaning "a skin or leather mat spread on the ground." While eating, people would sit on the floor with their legs folded under them or in the position of kneeling.

**802. A blessing was said** by each person after the master of the house said it, such as "In the name of God," or "God be praised." Only after all had said the blessing did they begin to eat by dipping or scooping with their bread in a common serving bowl. The only dishes used were those in which the food was placed on the table; there were no individual dishes for those dining. Gideon put the meat in a basket, and the broth in a pot (Judg. 6:19). Meat was generally eaten with the fingers.

**803. A prayer of thanks** was said at the end of the meal. Deuteronomy 8:10 states: "When you have eaten and are satisfied, praise the LORD your God for the good land he has given you." It was customary for one of the guests to give the thanks in a loud voice, and for the rest to say, "Amen."

**804. The Hebrew families** looked to the promise God originally gave to them about health for their bodies throughout their wilderness experiences and after they were in the Promised Land. "If you listen carefully to the voice of the LORD your God and do what is right in his eyes, if you pay attention to his commands and keep all his decrees, I will not bring on you any of the diseases I brought on the Egyptians, for I am the LORD, who heals you" (Exod. 15:26). Health was promised if they were obedient to the law of God.

## SICKNESS AND DEATH

**805. Sickness could be expected** when God's law was disobeyed, according to the law. The twenty-eighth chapter of Deuteronomy lists many curses that would come upon the children of Israel because of disobedience. Therefore the Israelites would grow up believing that health was a reward for obedience and sickness came as punishment. The ancient Hebrews did not go to physicians when they were ill. There are surprisingly few references to doctors in the Old Testament times, and it's possible that those mentioned were foreigners (2 Chron. 16:12; Job 13:4; Jer. 8:22).

**806. Multitudes of sick people in the land** are described in the New Testament Gospel records. Many were brought to Jesus to be healed. In the days before the British occupied the land and before the modern Jews brought in scientific medical skills, the land of Israel was overrun with all kinds of afflicted people. While traveling through the land, one would hardly be out of sight of blind beggars, crippled people, or lepers.

**807. The Jews of the New Testament** lacked knowledge of medicine, so they would seek help from the most pious man for healing power, rather than the most educated. They believed sickness was punishment for the sin of the sick person or a relative. Concerning the blind man, the disciples asked Jesus, "Rabbi, who sinned, this man or his parents, that he was born blind?" (John 9:2).

**808. Mark adds an interesting fact** in his account of Christ healing the woman with an issue of blood. He says that she "had suffered a great deal under the care of many doctors and had spent all she had" (Mark 5:26). One scholar of the Talmud of Babylon suggests that some of the rabbis posed as physicians and some prescribed very queer remedies for a woman with this type of ailment. If one procedure didn't succeed, another one was suggested.

**809. As soon as a death took place,** a wail was raised to announce to all the neighborhood what had happened. This was a sign for the relatives to begin their grieving. The death wail is described as a sharp, shrill, ear-piercing shriek. This shriek is followed by prolonged wails. This death wail was referred to in connection with the death of all the firstborn in Egypt. "Pharaoh and all his officials and all the Egyptians got up during the night, and there was loud wailing in Egypt, for there was not a house without someone dead" (Exod. 12:30).

**810. Relatives and friends continued their laments** from the time the death wail was heard until the burial. The prophet Micah compared it to the cry of wild beasts or birds. During these lamentations, loved ones exclaimed their sorrow, repeating words over and over as David did when he mourned the death of Absalom: "O my son Absalom! My son, my son Absalom! If only I had died instead of you—O Absalom, my son, my son!" (2 Sam. 18:33).

**811. Professional mourners,** who were called in at the time of sorrow to express mourning for the dead, are mentioned by the Hebrew prophets: "Call for the mourning women, that they may come; . . . And let them make haste, and take up a wailing for us (Jer. 9:17–18 KJV). Professional wailers were hired like singers would be for a Western funeral.

**812. Sackcloth was worn,** and they often tore their garments in order to let people know the depth of their grief (2 Sam. 3:31). Even today mourners will cry freely and beat their breasts to express sorrow. It is interesting to note, however, that priests were not allowed to rip their clothes even to mourn a parent's death.

**813. Burial follows death quickly,** usually the same day. The people of these regions have a primitive idea that the spirit of the one who dies hovers near the body for three days after death. Mourners believe this spirit is able to hear the wailing calls of grief. Martha, no doubt, thought it would be hopeless to think of reviving her brother's body, because he had been dead four days (John 11:39).

**814. Three classes of Arabs** are found in Palestine. The nomad or bedouin Arabs are shepherds who live in tents. The peasant or fellahin Arabs are farmers and usually live in villages in one-room houses. City or belladin Arabs do business in the larger cities. The belladin Arabs have come in contact with Western civilization and their manners and customs have undergone many changes. The peasant farmers, however, have changed customs very little and the bedouins have adopted almost no changes.

# 25

# Culture Shock between the Ages

**815. The Bible speaks about miracles** without making apology or even changing its tone. In other words, it doesn't anticipate skepticism. It considers the whole creation rather miraculous. Its writers show the same awe for a sunrise as for a day when the sun stands still.

**816. Male-female relationships in the Bible do**—compared to our present-day standards—put women in a subordinate position to men. But when the Bible is compared to the standards of the day in which it was written, it continually gave women a better place in life than that culture allowed them.

**817. A modern atheist** says that he or she doesn't believe in God—not gods. Antiquity knew no such atheists. Everyone and every nation had a god of their own, and usually more than one. The proclamation of monotheism must have sounded very strange to the surrounding cultures of that time.

**818. The issue of intermarriage** is still a divisive and emotional question among contemporary Jews because it defines who is a Jew. According to Jewish law, a Jew is one who is born to a Jewish mother or is converted to Judaism.

**819. The Mosaic law allowed polygamy** (more than one wife) among the Hebrew people. Wives were given certain protections against abuses and there were various regulations regarding these marriages. There was among the Israelites, however, a marked tendency toward monogamy (only one wife). The main reason may have been that the custom of having more than one wife was too expensive for most people.

**820. The Mosaic law** did forbid multiple wives for the kings of Israel with the warning that the king's heart would be led astray (Deut. 17:17). The cause of much trouble in the lives of David and Solomon, as well as Ahab, was that they followed the example of the kings in their day of taking many heathen wives, rather than obeying God's law. Men like Adam, Noah, Isaac, Joseph, Moses, and Job had only one wife.

**821. In the East the custom of arranged marriages** goes back to early Old Testament times. When Esau married against his parents' wishes, he caused Isaac and Rebekah grief. Why did parents insist on their right to select a bride for their son? The new bride became a member of the bridegroom's clan, and the whole family had a vested interested in knowing if she would be a good fit. There is evidence that sometimes the son or daughter was consulted, as in Rebekah's case when she was asked if she was willing to go and become the wife of Isaac (Gen. 24:58).

**822. What's love got to do with it?** Eastern peoples consider love between husband and wife very much like westerners do between brother and sister. It is believed that husbands and wives should love one another because God chose them for each other through the selection of their parents. Love comes after marriage. There are some exceptions to the rule. The case of Jacob and Rachel is the most notable example. For Jacob it was love at first sight (Gen. 29:10–18).

**823. For centuries it has been possible for a husband in Arab lands** to divorce his wife by a spoken word. When the wife is divorced, she is entitled to all her wearing apparel, and the husband cannot take anything from her that she has on her body. For this reason, coins on the headgear, rings, and necklaces became an important source of wealth in time of a woman's need. Such customs of divorce were no doubt prevalent in Gentile lands during Old Testament times. A woman was not allowed to divorce her husband.

**824. A husband must give a written certificate of divorce** (Deut. 24:1) to his wife in order to divorce her. This is so that she may remarry. The prophet Malachi taught that God hated divorce and severely condemned any man who dealt treacherously with the wife of his covenant (Mal. 2:14–16).

**825. The sin of adultery** did not have anything to do with divorce under the Jewish law. Adultery was punishable by death or stoning (Lev. 20:10). A man who was guilty of unfaithfulness was considered a criminal only in that he had invaded the rights of another man. Jesus swept away all grounds for divorce under the law, and made unfaithfulness the lone grounds for divorce for New Testament Christians (Matt. 5:31–32).

**826. Prostitutes** often appear in the stories of the Bible. There were two kinds of prostitutes in the Hebrew Scriptures. There were "cultic prostitutes" of the Canaanite religion, but Rahab, the prostitute in Jericho, was a *zonah*, which is Hebrew for a common prostitute. Rahab was the prostitute who hid the Israelite spies and later dangled a red cord out her window to mark her house for protection during the conquest of Jericho. New Testament genealogy in Matthew lists Rahab as the mother of Boaz, who married Ruth and is an ancestor of David, as well as Jesus.

**827. Jesus took no public stand** against slavery, racism, class warfare, state-sponsored terrorism, military occupation, or corruption in government in the Gospels. He spoke not a word against abortion or infanticide, homosexuality or the exploitation of women and children. Of all the social evils of his day, Jesus spoke out against the Pharisees and their spiritual corruption.

**828. One sacrifice that only the women** gave to the Lord was offered after the birth of a child: "When the days of her purification for a son or daughter are over, she is to bring to the priest at the entrance to the Tent of Meeting a year-old lamb for a burnt offering and a young pigeon or a dove for a sin offering" (Lev. 12:6).

**829. Jewish women were perhaps less active** in temple or synagogue worship than later in history. Although there was a special area at the temple known as the "court of women," women were not allowed to go into the inner court. Sources other than the Bible indicate that women did not read the Torah or recite prayers in the synagogue, but they could sit and listen in the special women's area.

**830. A different picture unfolds in the early Christian church.** Luke 8:1–3 indicates that Jesus welcomed some women as traveling companions. He encouraged Martha and Mary to sit at his feet as disciples.

**831. After Jesus ascended into heaven,** several women met with the other disciples in the upper room to pray. Both men and women gathered at the home of John Mark's mother to pray for the release of Peter; and both men and women prayed regularly in the church at Corinth (which is why Paul gave instructions to both men and women about how to pray in public).

# 26

# Angels in the Bible

**832. The word *angel*** comes from the Greek word *aggelos* (pronounced angelos) and means "messenger." In the Bible this is the form used in almost every mention of angels except one—in Luke 20:36 (KJV) where the phrase reads "equal unto the angels," or the Greek word *isaggelos,* which means "like an angel or "angelic."

**833. Angels are** beings that are created as "intermediate" beings between God and man. They are created beings by God, making them lower, but Psalm 8:5 states that man was made a little lower than the angels.

**834. There are more than three hundred** references to angels in the Bible. They play an important role and are seen in some of the most famous Bible stories, including the Christmas story.

**835. An angel is neither a god nor a human.** Angels are spirits, as Hebrews says: "[they are] ministering spirits sent to serve those who will inherit salvation."

185

**836. The first mention of angels in the Bible** is when Adam and Eve left the Garden after the fall. They are banished from Eden, and Eden is protected by cherubim, angels that are depicted elsewhere as winged bulls or lions with human heads.

**837. Cherubim are symbolic** attendants to places of the Lord's "enthronement" on earth in the Old Testament. They guard the Garden of Eden and the ark of the covenant.

**838. People had forgotten what cherubim signified** by Jesus' time, and the historian Josephus wrote in the first century A.D. that "no one can tell what they were like." Now archaeology has unearthed much of the forgotten past of the biblical world, and it is believed that a cherub was a small wing-bearing lion with a human head, in other words a sphinx. This was the winged creature most often portrayed in Canaanite art, and Canaanite kings are often shown seated on thrones supported by two cherubim. The Israelites may have adapted the cherubim to make a throne for the invisible presence of God.

**839. Angels have three important responsibilities:** to attend God's holy throne, to protect people, and to serve as messengers carrying special news or tidings. They are worshipful beings that serve God by carrying out his wishes through these three main roles.

**840. Daniel gives a prophetic picture** of what attending the throne of the Almighty God appears like:

> The Ancient of Days took his seat.
> His clothing was as white as snow;
>     the hair of his head was white like wool. . . .
> A river of fire was flowing,
>     coming out from before him.
> Thousands upon thousands attended him;
>     ten thousand times ten thousand stood before him.
>
> Daniel 7:9–10

Angels are all around God, worshiping him.

**841. Guardian angels** are spoken of throughout the Bible. Abraham spoke of God sending his angel before his servant Elias as the steward went to seek out a wife for Abraham's son Isaac. Psalm 91:11–12 also speaks of watchful angels:

> For he will command his angels concerning you
>    to guard you in all your ways;
> they will lift you up in their hands,
>    so that you will not strike your foot against a stone.

**842. As messengers** the angels communicate God's will to us. They serve as rescuers (such as when Lot was saved from Sodom); as bearers of great tidings (to Mary concerning the birth of Jesus); to instruct prophets (Daniel was given detailed direction from "the man Gabriel"). Angels are mediators who pass along messages God has for his people.

**843. Hebrews 1:14 says** angels are "ministering spirits sent to serve those who will inherit salvation." As such they come to our aid and offer help where they can to make our lives better. They are spiritual beings that remain invisible.

**844. A "heavenly host"** is not merely a bunch of angels. The term means an "angel army." The heavenly host that came upon the shepherds when Jesus was born was singing and praising God, but they were a "company" of God's army of angels nonetheless.

**845. Jacob's vision** depicts the angels as being lined up on an immense ladder that stretches between the earth and the heavens (Gen. 28:12–15). God looks down and sees us and watches as the angels bring their messages from him.

**846. There is a hierarchical organization** of angels, though it is uncertain exactly what that might look like. There are seven angels in God's presence that surround the throne. These angels are constantly worshiping their Creator.

**847. Saint Denis the Areopagite** wrote a treatise called "De Coelesti Hierarchia" that claims there are defined levels and ranks of angels. However, his work was largely unaccepted except for that pertaining to choirs of angels. The church heartily accepts this idea but does not make believing in varying levels of angels a requirement.

**848. Gregory the Great** demonstrated what the early church believed concerning angels with his comments: "There are nine orders of angels, viz., Angels, Archangels, Virtues, Powers, Principalities, Dominations, Throne, Cherubim, and Seraphim." He based this on the apostle Paul's findings as well as other Scriptures.

**849. The apostle Paul** tells us four of the orders of angels in his letter to the Ephesians: "above all principality, and power, and might, and dominion" (KJV). He also writes to the Colossians concerning angels: "whether they be thrones, or dominions, or principalities, or powers."

**850. Saint Thomas,** who was also from the early church, divided the angels into three hierarchies with three orders of angels in each. Where they are in terms of God himself is the main basis for the divisions. The seraphim, cherubim, and thrones are in the first one; the dominations, virtues, and powers in the second; and the principalities, archangels, and angels are in the third and final hierarchy.

**851. Only two personal names** for angels are given in the Bible: Michael and Gabriel. Other angels with personal names are given in the Apocrypha, such as Uriel and Jeremiel.

**852. Gabriel** makes appearances in both the Old and New Testaments. He interprets Daniel's visions in the Book of Daniel and also announces the births of John and Jesus to their respective parents.

**853. Michael is an archangel** and a warrior in the angelic realm. He is the protector of Israel, according to several references in the Book of Daniel and one in the Book of Revelation.

**854. Fallen angels** are angels who have rebelled against God and lost their standing in heaven. They have not been cast into hell, and they are under God's power, but they take orders from Satan (Rev. 12:7).

**855. The Nephilim** are a people spoken of in Genesis 6. Some believe this people of great strength were the result of fallen angels marrying the daughters of men on earth to produce offspring of unusual size and strength. The Bible calls these people "the heroes of old, men of renown." God did not look with favor on the actions of these angels, and their offspring were eventually wiped out with the flood.

**856. Satan is perhaps the most famous angel** of all time. He is a fallen angel, one who was cast out of heaven after rebelling against God. Paul speaks of how Satan "masquerades as an angel of light" (2 Cor. 11:14). In reality Satan is "the prince of darkness."

**857. A final battle between the good angels and the fallen angels** is prophesied in Revelation 12:7–9: "And there was war in heaven. Michael [archangel] and his angels fought against the dragon, and the dragon and his angels fought back. But he was not strong enough, and they lost their place in heaven. The great dragon was hurled down—that ancient serpent called the devil, or Satan, who leads the whole world astray. He was hurled to the earth, and his angels with him."

**858. Christians will see angels** on the last day. Matthew 24:31 states that God will "send his angels with a loud trumpet call, and they will gather his elect from the four winds, from one end of the heavens to the other." Angels will escort believers into heaven and to the holy throne!

# 27

# The Animal Kingdom

**859. The Bible is full of animal references.** About eighty species of mammals are named, about twenty-five kinds of birds, eight types of reptiles and amphibians, and a dozen insects. We now know that many other living things inhabit these lands besides those named in the Bible. Yet this knowledge of approximately 125 kinds of animals reveals how remarkably familiar these ancient people were with the living things around them.

**860. Sheep** were the most important domestic animals of the Hebrews. Both goats and sheep provided meat, but the sheep was preferred for its wool and the goat furnished milk. Sheep were generally only eaten for sacrifices. The sheep is named more often in the Bible than any other animal—more than four hundred times.

**861. The goat** may have been the earliest food animal to be domesticated by man, and that probably took place in the vicinity of Jericho about nine thousand years ago. The only animal domesticated earlier was the dog! The goat is mentioned nearly two hundred times. Goats were especially appreciated for their ability to live on rough land and forage in difficult areas.

**862. Cattle** are actually descended from a wild breed of ox. They were used early on in the Bible for their milk, although the bulls were eventually prized even more for their abilities to carry heavy loads. Cows even carried the ark of the covenant back to Israel (1 Sam. 6:7)!

**863. Cows are much more difficult to keep** than sheep and goats. Cattle require more care, as well as a constant food supply, when they are in permanent settlements. Because Abraham lived much of his life as a nomad, he may have maintained cows, but certainly not as many as his sheep and goats.

**864. The first mention of the donkey, or ass,** in the Bible occurs when it is stated that the Pharaoh of Egypt presented Abraham with several donkeys as gifts (Gen. 12:16). To the Egyptian, as in Abraham's culture, the donkey was solely a means of transporting goods. Only later was it used for riding, pulling the plow, and turning millstones to grind grain.

**865. The domesticated donkey** is one of the world's most useful animals. And it certainly was to the Hebrews. Numerous laws were given about their treatment, which testifies to the important place they held in the Hebrew economy. A donkey had to be rested on the Sabbath, and one that had fallen under the weight of its burden had to be helped.

**866. Abraham used donkeys in his caravans** long before camels were on the scene.

**867. The Hebrews were the only people in the ancient world recorded as riding on donkeys.** And only the common people did so. It was considered humiliating for a ruler to ride on one. Biblical kings such as David are recorded as riding on mules (the hybrid mix of a male donkey and a female horse) or in chariots pulled by horses, but never on donkeys. So when Jesus rode on a donkey, it was a symbol of his humility.

**868. Donkeys go long periods without water,** work hard in hot climates, and survive on a minimum amount of food. Also a donkey's milk is extremely nutritious, closely resembling human milk in its chemical composition.

**869. Horses** were used largely for battle purposes. They were a war symbol of power and strength. They weren't as strong or as capable as the donkeys, camels, and cattle to serve as beasts of burden.

**870. Jericho,** an imposing fortress near where the Jordan enters the Dead Sea, stood in the way of the Israelites, but with the blasts of the ram's horn, or *shofar,* the walls tumbled down. Ancient breeds of sheep often grew huge horns from which musical instruments were made. The horn was heated with steam until it was soft enough for its natural curve to be straightened out. Then the wide end where the horn had been attached to the ram was bent at almost a right angle.

**871. The camel had not yet reached Egypt** when Abraham visited, according to the findings of archaeologists. It was common in the Fertile Crescent where Abraham's servant was sent to find a bride for his son Isaac. In Genesis 24:12–21, the servant came upon Rebekah who, in offering to water the servant's camels, showed herself to be God's choice for Isaac.

**872. The biblical camel is the one-humped kind,** often called a dromedary. Camels are desirable animals only to people who live in deserts because they are excellently adapted to the conditions there. But most of the ancient world preferred other beasts of burden such as donkeys, horses, and oxen. The camel has only one baby every three years, and sometimes fewer than that. Its ability to learn is meager, and it is impossible to train one to respond as well as a horse. It is so bad tempered (especially the males) that Roman soldiers kept them outside the walls of their posts.

**873. It is true that a thirsty camel** can drink enormous amounts of water very fast, about twenty-five gallons in approximately ten minutes. It is also true that a camel can travel four days without taking a single drink of water. It is not true, however, that water is stored in its hump. The camel's hump actually stores food. It is a mass of muscle around which fat accumulates. A camel can be fed at the beginning of a trip and not again until the end. After a long, hard journey, the hump shrinks and it flops to one side.

**874. It is completely untrue that a camel has a special sense of direction** in the trackless desert. In fact camels easily lose their way and often become separated from the rest of their caravans.

**875. Locusts** are insects, the most-mentioned insect in the whole Bible. They destroy crops and plague people. They were one of the plagues sent upon Egypt by God before Pharaoh let the people go out of the land. Some think they were permitted as food, however, because John the Baptist ate locusts and honey while staying in the wilderness (Mark 1:6).

**876. Insects** such as ants and honeybees were well-respected in the Bible. Ants are busy animals and work hard to stay organized; Proverbs rewards the ant by giving it a place in Scripture. Honey was a special commodity in the Middle East, and honeybees were prized.

**877. Flies, fleas, and gnats** (also translated "lice") were disliked strongly and could also carry disease. As in modern times, such insects were greatly unappreciated. They were a plague that descended on Egypt when Pharaoh remained stubborn about letting the Israelites leave.

**878. Lions** were kept by royalty and remain a sign of wealth and power. The regal beasts were a common enough animal in the Old Testament, but they have since become extinct in the Middle East. Killing a lion was a sign of great strength, as evidenced by David and Samson when they slew the majestic beasts.

**879. The bear** is given little mention in the Bible. However, they were perhaps feared more than lions (Amos 5:19). Researchers believe the references are to the Syrian brown bear, a species found today in certain parts of the Bible region. The young children who mocked Elisha because of his baldness were eaten by bears.

**880. Behemoth . . . or hippopotamus?** In a long series of verses in chapter 40 of the Book of Job, the main character describes an animal he calls a "behemoth," but it is very likely a hippopotamus. Hippopotami may have inhabited the Jordan Valley in biblical times, although none are found there now. The Hebrews knew them in Egypt, and it is even possible that Job's behemoth is derived from the Egyptian name for this animal—*pehemau,* which means "ox of the water."

**881. An unknown beast.** Job goes to great length (thirty-four verses in chapter 41) identifying the "leviathan." Commentators on the Bible disagree as to whether the leviathan was a crocodile, a whale, or even some mythical animal. Most likely Job had in mind a crocodile, although his description includes fire spouting from its mouth.

**882. The "beasts of the earth"** that Jeremiah said would appear after the destruction of Judah probably referred to wild dogs and hyenas. Today dogs are known as "man's best friend," but during biblical times packs of snarling dogs foraged through the city streets and even dug up corpses to feed on them. When Jezebel's body was eaten by dogs after her death, it was a sign of utter humiliation.

**883. The striped hyena** is found in the Holy Land and was the most feared and detested of the animal kingdom in the ancient world, due to its habit of digging up graves. The only people who did not hold this strong aversion to hyenas were the Egyptians, who domesticated them for a source of food. Young hyenas are easy to tame and quickly become attached to their masters.

**884. The red fox,** an animal we regard as exceedingly clever, won no praise from Solomon. Every reference to it in the Bible is contemptuous. Because they scavenged like wild dogs and hyenas, in the Israelite cities foxes were killed quickly. They feed on almost anything: rodents, eggs, insects, and grass. They even eat fruit, which may explain Solomon's reference to "the little foxes that ruin the vineyards" (Song of Sol. 2:15).

**885. Pigs** were unclean and not domesticated by the Hebrews. They are mentioned, but the references are always negative. Jesus drew demons into a herd of pigs, and the prodigal son who squanders everything and ends up tending to pigs has reached the very lowest level of employment.

**886. Ravens and crows** were common birds. The raven was the first bird to leave the ark (Gen. 8:6–7). Elijah was fed by ravens while he was hiding from enemies (1 Kings 17:6).

**887. The ostrich** was abundant in the Arabian Desert in Job's time, but it became extinct there during World War II. Job paints a vivid word picture of the ostrich in chapter 39 (vv. 14–17).

**888. The crane** is tall and stately with a wingspread of about eight feet. It is the largest migrating bird to fly over the Holy Land. Its mass flights are dramatic because the birds number in the thousands, and also because they make a trumpeting sound that fills the air. One of the loudest sounds made by any bird, it is produced by the crane's extremely long windpipe, which is coiled like a French horn.

**889. The earliest statements about bird migrations** came from Jeremiah. No one in the ancient world, however, seemed to know for sure where migrating birds came from, why they left, or where they flew next. "Even the stork in the sky knows her appointed seasons; and the dove, the swift and the thrush observe the time of their migration" (Jer. 8:7). The white stork is unmistakable in flight because of its sharply pointed head and extended neck, long dangling legs, and slowly flapping wings. Flocks of several thousand of them pass over the Holy Land at a time.

**890. Sparrows** were eaten as food. They were carefully hunted and sold in the marketplace. Jesus spoke of two sparrows being sold for a farthing.

**891. Jonah was swallowed by "a great fish."** There has been considerable dispute, however, about what sea creature is large enough to swallow anything the size of a human. A likely creature that swallowed Jonah is a true fish—the man-eating white shark, often found in the Mediterranean. This shark is extremely large, occasionally up to sixty feet in length, and it is quite capable of swallowing a human. It can also store food in its belly for many days without digesting it.

**892. Snakes,** or serpents, are part of the reptile family and receive some mention in the Bible. Satan appeared as a serpent to Eve in the Garden of Eden. Moses held up a brass serpent figure to cure the bites of snakes on the people. Later it became a worshiped object. Interestingly most of the references found in the New Testament are metaphorical rather than literal.

**893. Lizards** are the most common reptile in the Bible region. They were an unclean creeping animal as described in Leviticus 11:29–39, and though common, they were not appreciated as a food source.

**894. The Israelites knew about monkeys** from their stay in Egypt, because the African baboon was sacred to the god Thoth and was sometimes even kept as a pet. The monkey brought back by Solomon's fleet possibly was the rhesus, the kind most often seen in zoos.

**895. Peacocks** were the last of the precious cargo mentioned from Ophir, and although the common peacock is native only to southern India and Ceylon, people have spread it around the world. It is hardy and can endure a wide range of climates and living conditions.

**896. The Israelites were familiar with quail,** for wall paintings in Egyptian tombs dating from the time of the Exodus show that people caught the birds in nets for food. However, they had probably never seen so many of them at one time as when God sent them quail in the wilderness (Exod. 16:13).

**897. Migratory quail** are short-winged and have only weak powers of flight. They are often blown off course by strong winds and fall exhausted onto the nearest land. God used this very process to cause quail to fall on the Israelite camp. The Bible states that there was a wind that brought the quail from the sea and that the quail fell to earth in the evening.

**898. The rooster was little different** from its wild-pheasant ancestor, the red jungle fowl. It was found from Pakistan to Java until recent decades, when new breeds of chickens were developed. The red jungle fowl closely resembles the barnyard chicken both in appearance and in habits, except that it can still fly.

**899. The chicken may have been domesticated** as early as fifty-two hundred years ago in India. The birds were raised at that time for the sport of cockfighting, and were not bred for food until several centuries before the time of Jesus.

# 28

# The Plant Kingdom

**900. Almond trees** were admired for their beautiful blossoms by the ancients. The pretty blooms were even used in artwork, such as on the ark (Exod. 25:33–34). The nuts and oil taken from the nuts were used for food. Almond blossoms had a special religious significance for the Hebrews, who in ancient times carved them on the golden candlesticks in the tabernacle, and who still carry them to this day to the synagogue for festivals.

**901. Apple trees** are only mentioned in two books of the Bible: Proverbs and Song of Solomon. As a result it is not clear if the "apple" tree was in fact apple-bearing or if perhaps the "apples" might have been apricots or even figs.

**902. Cedar trees** came from Lebanon and were greatly prized for their height, strength, and the durability of the wood. The temples of early Israel utilized the mighty trees for their buildings. Cedar wood is mentioned for use in cleansing rituals, but it is now believed that specific reference was actually to a different type of wood, Phoenician juniper.

**903. Solomon had the tall cedars felled** by the thousands to supply timber for the temple and for his fabulous palace, which he named "the House of the Forest of Lebanon." He sent shifts of ten thousand Israelites a month to aid the native workers in cutting down the forests.

**904. Only barren slopes remain** where the cedars used to be. Only a few scattered groves survived the axes of empire after empire. One small grove is preserved in a park about eighty miles north of Beirut, Lebanon.

**905. Cutting down an olive tree actually rejuvenates it.** At the time of cutting, new and more vigorous sprouts grow up out of the roots. The roots are extremely long-lived, and it is almost impossible to kill an olive tree merely by chopping it down. The olive was the symbol of peace in the ancient world, and so it was fitting that it was associated with Jesus, who was known as the Prince of Peace.

**906. Solomon built smelters, a shipyard, and a port** at Eziongeber (today known as Elath). His smelters were located in a seemingly unlikely place, an inhospitable desert where water was scarce. There was good reason for building them there, however. The smelters utilized some of the principles of the modern blast furnace. A constant and powerful wind roars down the valley where Solomon's smelters stood, and it acted as bellows that kept the furnace fires burning at high temperatures.

**907. Forest trees** served as a symbol of holiness to the Israelites. The names of both the oak and the terebinth, the two most common forest trees of the Holy Land, were derived from Hebrew words meaning "God." David's son Solomon, in the fourth year of his reign, began work on the magnificent temple at Jerusalem. The walls of the temple were built of marble, but they were roofed and lined inside with wood from the cedar of Lebanon.

**908. Oak trees** were used as burial places (Gen. 35:8; 1 Chron. 10:12). Three species of the oak tree grow in Palestine; it is believed the tabor oak is the one referred to in Scripture.

**909. Palm trees** were especially abundant in the Jordan valley, and Jericho was known as the city of palm trees. Symbolically the trees were used to depict grace. The date palm also symbolized rejoicing; when Jesus made his triumphal entry into Jerusalem, the crowds waved palm branches to celebrate and honor him.

**910. Sycamore trees** vary from continent to continent. Those talked about in the Bible (Egypt and Palestine) are sturdy ever-green trees that bear figs. The Egyptians cultivated it for lumber as well as for its fruit, but in Israel it was mainly grown for the fruit. The sycamore tree is perhaps best remembered for its helping Zaccheus, a short man, see Jesus as he passed by.

**911. Willow trees** generally grow near streams in the Middle East. Most Bible references to the trees associate them with water as a result—"the willow of the brook" for instance.

**912. The tree of the knowledge of good and evil** is perhaps the most notorious tree in history. The only source of temptation for Adam and Eve in the Garden was the tree from which God had told them not to eat.

**913. The castor oil plant** grows and withers quickly, especially when handled, and some believe it may be the "gourd" plant Jonah refers to in Jonah 4. The spiky, dark green leaves and reddish, yarn-ball blooms do not make gourds, however.

**914. The city of Ashkelon** was famed in the ancient world for the profusion of fruits and vegetables that grew in its fertile soil. One vegetable was the small onion or scallion, for which the city became noted in Roman times. Our word *scallion* comes from the Latin *caepa Ascalonia,* which means "onion of Ashkelon."

**915. Hyssop** is mentioned in the Bible on many occasions, but no plant we know of today by that name is a native species of the Middle East. It is thought that the plant referred to might be the herb marjoram, which is fragrant and comes from Syria.

**916. The lily,** though mentioned often in the Bible, is most likely not the common flower that goes by that name.

**917. Mandrakes** are a flowering herb that bears fruit in the spring. They are said to have powers and can serve as an aphrodisiac, which we know from Leah and Rachel's quarrel over their husband, Jacob, visiting their separate tents and whether it was worth sharing some mandrakes in order to promote conception.

**918. Myrtle** has beautiful pink blossoms with a delicate fragrance; the leaves are also quite fragrant. The myrtle was used by Isaiah as a symbol of God's continuous care and provision of Israel (Isa. 41:19–20). The branches were used for festivals as well (Neh. 8:15–16).

**919. Roses** are not native to the Bible lands, and so it is unlikely that the blooms we know as roses actually grew there. More likely other flowers were being referred to. Roses are mentioned several times in the apocryphal books and once in Song of Solomon.

**920. Wormwood** is used to symbolize bitterness because it has a unique bitter taste. The plant has many species that grow in Palestine. It is almost more of a shrub, though it can grow quite tall. It is in the same plant family as mugwort and western sagebrush. These plants all have a bitter taste and a strong odor. The Hebrews thought of bitter things as poisonous and thus as symbols of calamity and sorrow, but they used wormwood as a seasoning, a tonic, and a worm medicine.

**921. Balm of Gilead** refers to a fragrant resin that is obtained from cuts in the bark of trees. It is used for both perfumes and medicines. Several different plants produce such resins, and no one is sure which one Jeremiah meant. It might have been the Jericho balsam, but a more likely possibility is liquidambar, which produces the gum known as storax or stacte, which is still used in medicine. It is almost identical to the tree Americans call red gum or sweet gum.

**922. Compared to the desert,** Canaan must have seemed like paradise, with its vineyards and its orchards of olives, figs, dates, and pomegranates. Next to the grape, the fig was the Israelites' most valued crop. It provided a large part of their daily food. Both figs and dates were eaten either fresh or dried. Fig fruits were also used medicinally; and the sheaths of date clusters provided a sap that was used to make a kind of wine as well as a syrup called "honey" in the Bible.

**923. Pomegranates** grow wild as large shrubs or small trees in many parts of the Near East. So important was this "apple with grains," filled with many red-colored, juicy seeds, to the Israelites that it was used as a design to decorate the temple and also coins in Jerusalem.

**924. Along the Nile and throughout the ancient Near East,** the most important grain crops were wheat and barley. Both grains have been cultivated in Egypt and the Near East since the earliest recorded times. The earliest evidence comes from near Mount Carmel, on the coast of northern Israel. It dates from about nine thousand years ago.

**925. In the Holy Land, barley** was mainly used to feed animals because its protein content was less than wheat. It was also the chief grain of the poor people and so it became a symbol of poverty. Barley was such a staple grain of the Hebrews that it furnished them with units of measurement—three barley grains laid end to end were equal to an inch, about twenty-four to a "span," and forty-eight to a "cubit" (about seventeen inches).

**926. The tall and graceful papyrus reed or bulrush** was one of the most abundant plants to grow along the banks of the Nile. At the top of its fifteen-foot stem is a plume of wispy stalks that resemble feathers. Papyrus furnished the world's first material for making paper. In fact our word *paper* is derived from it. The stem was pressed flat under heavy weights until it dried. It was then cut into sheets of suitable size, which were polished with ivory to make a smooth writing surface. Sometimes sheets were glued or sewn together to make long rolls of paper, usually about thirty feet long. One roll has been discovered that is 130 feet in length! Each end of the roll was attached to a handle to make winding easier.

**927. In Jesus' parable of the prodigal son,** the younger of two sons squandered his half of the inheritance. He then became so poor that he would fill his belly with the husks that the swine ate (Luke 15:16). Husks came from the pods of the carob tree, also commonly called the locust, which were fed to farm animals.

**928. The carob tree grows beans in a pod** that resemble our green peas. Today in the Near East the pods provide fodder for animals and food for very poor people, although in Jesus' time humans did not eat them unless they were as famished as the prodigal son.

**929. Some think that the "locust"** (Matt. 3:4) John the Baptist ate in the wilderness was not the insect but rather the pod from the carob tree. For this reason the carob is sometimes called "Saint John's bread tree."

**930. Few plants in the Holy Land have seeds smaller** than the mustard seed. As Jesus points out in his parable in Matthew 13, mustard often grows as large as a tree, reaching a height of about fifteen feet, with a stalk as thick as a man's arm. Mustard was widely cultivated in the Middle East for the flavor of its seed.

**931. References to the grapevine abound in Scripture.** It is a plant so widely cultivated in the Holy Land that it was known to all. The grapevine is one of the very first plants mentioned in the Bible (one of Noah's first jobs after the flood was to plant a vineyard) and its image appears some two hundred times in both the Old and New Testaments. The grape has been cultivated for so long that its origin is shrouded in mystery.

**932. The date palm** was a sign of majesty and fruitfulness to people of the Holy Land. The huge leaves were symbols of triumph and were often carried in ceremonies, but they were also used for roofing, fencing, and the making of mats, baskets, and dishes. Rope was made from the fibrous material in the crown of the trees. The trunk was used for timber, and the date fruit was food for animals as well as people. It is said that the date palm has more uses than the year has days.

**933. The shrub commonly known as "crown of thorns,"** grown in many European and American gardens, could not possibly be the one mentioned in the Bible. This plant is native to the island of Madagascar and it was unknown in the Holy Land in Jesus' time. Many scholars now believe that the crown was made from a straggly shrub often called the Jerusalem thorn. It grows abundantly around Jerusalem, and its twigs are flexible enough to be woven.

# 29

# Music in the Bible

**934. Musical instruments as well as human melody** are mentioned all through the Bible. The Hebrew culture included music; it was in fact an important part of their daily lives. Music was used for both sacred and secular occasions.

**935. "The father of all who play the harp and flute."** Jubal was the son of Lamech and a descendant of Cain, but his main title was that of music patriarch (Gen. 4:21).

**936. Music was played at all occasions,** such as at religious festivals and worship services, at funerals (Matt. 9:23), in battle (Exod. 15:20–21; 2 Chron. 20:28), and even just to pass the time while shepherds watched their sheep. David was a talented harpist. There are instances of music in royal settings as well as very humble ones in the Bible. It doesn't appear to be an aspect of culture that was truly only for one segment of society.

**937. Instruments** ranged in types and styles, but the necessary elements for an orchestra were present: strings, wind instruments, and a percussion section. Though instruments could certainly be played alone, orchestras did exist. David was said to have four thousand instrumentalists organized for his musical needs and requests.

**938. The "pipe" instrument** mentioned in Scripture was perhaps an oboe. The pipe would have been used in festivals and other times of rejoicing, as well as funerals and sad occasions. The prophet Jeremiah once compared the soulful, haunting sound to a sad heart (Jer. 48:36).

**939. The organ** is another wind instrument from Bible times, though it may have been a generic term for all wind instruments (Gen. 4:21 KJV).

**940. Trumpets** referred to a variety of different wind instruments—everything from a ram's horn to Moses' silver trumpet may correctly be classified within this instrument family. Another name used was "cornet."

**941. The flute** is only mentioned once in the King James Version of the Bible, in Daniel 3:5, but it is mentioned more in other, newer translations, such as the NIV (three times). It very well may have referred to a reed flute or some other instrument that closely resembles a modern flute.

**942. The harp** is perhaps the most-mentioned instrument in the Bible. It is believed that the instrument actually refers to the lyre, a similar stringed instrument of smaller proportions. The lyre was made of wood and had between eight and ten strings to pluck. The fingers or some sort of pick may have been used. The instrument may be of Syrian origin.

**943. Harps and heaven?** Many people associate heaven and harps. Many people don't realize that this connection actually comes from the Bible. The apostle John describes this in his vision, seeing the heavenly throne in the Book of Revelation.

**944. A psaltery** is another kind of harp, as is a viol. These were even smaller wooden-framed harps, and they would have been plucked with the fingers to make music. They may have been of

Phoenician origin. The Bible mentions these in 1 Samuel 10:5 and Isaiah 5:12.

**945. The sackbut,** despite the funny name, is a type of harp with a triangular shape. It has been mistranslated (Dan. 3:5) in various versions, but it is a harp.

**946. Cymbals** are a percussion instrument. They were used both in celebration and at ceremonies such as the dedication of the wall of Jerusalem (Neh. 12:27). There were two kinds of cymbals. The first had flat metal plates that were struck together to make a clashing, crashing noise. The other kind had one cymbal that was held stationary while the other one was banged against it.

**947. Timbrels,** or tambourines, are instruments still in use today. The bells and other "jingly" sounds come from light pieces of metal that shake and rattle together when the wood they are attached to is shaken or beat. The timbrel was used for happy occasions and to make music for singing and dancing.

# 30

# Symbols

**948. The cross** is perhaps the most recognized symbol of the Christian. Jesus was crucified on a cross between two criminals. His hands and feet were nailed into the cross, signs to forever remain that demonstrate the atoning work he performed on the cross for believers.

**949. The hand of God** is perhaps the most ancient symbol of God the Father. Like most symbols, it is referenced from Scripture. The meaning of the symbol relates to the creative power of God. Through his handiwork came forth the genius of creation.

**950. A crown** is a representation of the office Christ holds as King. The Scriptures teach that he is the "King of kings." The Bible also refers to Jesus as the "Crown of Life," which all who believe may take for themselves.

**951. The lantern** is a symbol of betrayal that comes directly from Scripture. When Judas came with the soldiers to arrest Jesus, the group carried torches and lanterns in order to find Jesus. Alternatively the lantern is a symbol of light.

**952. Jesus is the Light of the world,** the source that brings life to a dead world. Furthermore Christ's two distinct natures, divine and human, are an important tenet of Christ being both God and man. The traditional symbol to display this doctrine is to light two candles during church services, with one on either side of a cross.

**953. The Good Shepherd** is a biblical reference to Jesus' description of himself in the Gospel of John. As the redeemer of his people, the sheep, Jesus watches over them, protects them, and provides for their way into the shelter.

**954. The Holy Spirit** is most often represented by a dove and recalls the story of Jesus' baptism from the Scriptures. After Jesus was baptized by John the Baptist, a dove descended and God spoke from heaven. This is one of very few symbols for the Third Person of the Trinity.

**955. The seven doves, seven lamps, and seven-pointed star** all represent the seven gifts of the Holy Spirit stated in the Book of Revelation. The seven gifts are strength, honor, glory, blessing, power, riches, and wisdom.

# 31

# Bible Trivia

**956. Though _Trinity_ is a common Christian term,** the Bible never mentions the Trinity as such. It was a doctrine developed much later when the church was more established.

**957. Dreams were often used as a means** for God to speak to his prophets and other favored children. Items within the dreams symbolized real events or people or even future happenings. Joseph's dream about wheat sheaves foretold the time when he would be powerful in Egypt and lead that people through a drought and famine.

**958. The doctrine known as "Immaculate Conception,"** the belief that Mary herself was conceived without sin, has no biblical justification. This belief began early in Christian history and was officially accepted as dogma essential to Roman Catholic beliefs by Pope Pius IX in 1854.

**959. Knowing the basics.** In a 1997 survey, the *London Sunday Times* found that only 34 percent of 220 Anglican priests could recite all of the Ten Commandments without help.

**960. Two separate creation stories are told in Genesis** (Gen. 1:1–2:3 and Gen. 2:4–25), but there is no mention of an apple in the Garden of Eden story.

**961. The original Hebrew word for "ark"** meant "box" or "chest" in English.

**962. Although the King James Version** is often associated with Shakespearean English, neither Moses nor Jesus is ever quoted as saying "thee" or "thou."

**963. Place names** in the Bible often came from the person or persons who settled the area. They would give it a special name to commemorate the occasion.

**964. Jericho is the world's oldest city.** It was founded about 3500 B.C.

**965. Polytheism,** the belief in more than one god, distinguishes our age from that of the Bible more than any other cultural issue.

**966. The name *Jesus*** is the Greek version of the name *Joshua.*

**967. David,** the shepherd, warrior, and king of Israel, broke half of the Ten Commandments, from what we are told in the Bible. More than likely he broke all ten!

**968. Frankincense and myrrh** are both fragrant resins imported from India, Arabia, or Africa. They were therefore costly and precious in the Holy Land.

**969. The star.** About the time of the birth of Jesus in Bethlehem, a phenomenon occurred in the night sky. There has been considerable dispute about what this bright star of Bethlehem may have been. Whatever the astronomical phenomenon was exactly, it did not go unobserved in the ancient home of astronomy, Mesopotamia. The wise men or magi who saw the star and believed that it heralded the birth of Jesus were probably astronomers.

**970.** *Magus* **is a Persian word** that referred to the priests of Persia, and from *magus* we get our English word *magic*. In the ancient world the priests who could predict eclipses and the motions of the planets must have seemed to possess magical powers.

**971. Samaritans** did not have a great reputation among Jews. They were not good neighbors. The Jews and Samaritans had a long and unhappy history. The Samaritans had first come into the land when the Assyrians conquered Israel. An offshoot sect, they followed the books of Moses but did not treat the rest of the Hebrew Scriptures as sacred. As a result bad blood grew between the groups.

**972. As archaeologists excavated** the mound of the ancient city of Jericho (about a mile or so northwest of the modern city), they found not one ancient city but instead successive cities, each built atop the ruins of the previous ones. Jericho is the oldest known town in the world. Above the first signs of human habitation, five cities were built in antiquity—and the fourth of these appears to be the one that was conquered by Joshua.

**973. Double walls** nearly thirty feet high, with each wall about six feet thick, were discovered by archaeologists at the Jericho site. It is clear that this city had a violent end. Sections of the wall crumbled, and there is evidence of fire so intense that it burned bricks and cracked stones.

**974. Shibboleth.** Jephthah's men fought and defeated the tribesmen of Ephraim (another Israelite tribe who did not help Jephthah in his battle with the Ammonites). If an Ephraimite tried to cross the Jordan, Jephthah's men would ask him to say "Shibboleth," a word that means either "ear of corn" or "flood torrent." But due to regional dialects, these men couldn't pronounce the "sh" sound, and said "sibboleth" instead. Forty-two thousand men with this speech deficiency died at the Jordan. A contemporary story is told from World War II in which Dutch resistance fighters were able to cull out Nazi infiltrators who couldn't pronounce a particular Dutch name. "Shibboleth" has since come to mean a word or catchphrase that is distinctive to one group.

**975. Hammurabi (meaning "westerner") was an Ammorite** who conquered several Sumerian cities and developed a small empire, making him the first king to elevate Babylon from a small town to a major power. Some scholars believe that Hammurabi—generally dated as king of Babylon from 1792–1750 B.C.—might be the mysterious King Amraphel, king of Shinar, mentioned in Genesis 14.

**976. Hammurabi is best remembered for a code of law,** set down toward the end of his reign on clay tables and on stelae, or stone pillars. Clear parallels as well as clear differences can be drawn between Hammurabi's code and the law Moses received from God on Mount Sinai. Sadly the tablets on which the Ten Commandments were written disappeared with the ark of the covenant, but Hammurabi's laws were uncovered by French archaeologists in the ancient city of Susa and remain on display in the Louvre in Paris.

**977. Towers known as ziggurats,** which literally means "houses that lift up their heads," were erected throughout the Babylonian Empire and were probably intended as stairways for men to ascend and meet the gods. A ziggurat resembles a pyramid, but its sides are steplike. In constructing the tower, the builders "had brick for stone, and slime had they for morter" (Gen. 11:3 KJV). The bricks were made from mud and the "slime" was asphalt, found all over the Iranian oil fields even today.

**978. Pottery, made from clay and baked in a kiln,** is one of the most durable materials ever made. Glass flakes away, metals corrode and rust, wood and fabrics are destroyed by dampness and insects. Pottery alone survives. Although a pottery jar can easily be shattered, the broken pieces or shards may last for centuries and give clues to when the pottery was made, who made it, and its relationship to pottery made by neighboring people.

**979. Archaeologists have studied the shards** discovered in the Negeb that date from about the time Abraham crossed it. All the pottery made throughout this vast area was almost exactly the same, revealing that those were settled times and that the people of the Negeb traded peacefully with one another.

**980. The Shema** is the central confession of the Jewish faith: "Hear, O Israel: The LORD our God, the LORD is one." It is originally found in Deuteronomy 6:4, and Jesus quoted it, saying that the verse that follows ("Love the LORD your God with all your heart and with all your soul and with all your strength") is the greatest commandment.

## DEAD SEA SCROLLS

**981. Muhammed ed Dib** was tending goats in the spring of 1947, while the British still controlled Palestine. In the arid hills that surround the northern Dead Sea shore, the young goatherd dropped a stone into a cave and heard it hit something. Investigating further, he found ancient clay pots filled with scrolls and scraps of old leather covered in mysterious writing. His accidental find was the beginning of one of the most momentous and controversial discoveries in history—the "Dead Sea Scrolls."

**982. Muhammed's find launched a wider search** of the surrounding area, called Qumran, approximately ten miles south of Jericho, on a plateau overlooking the Dead Sea. Over the years many more scrolls and remnants of scrolls were uncovered. It was soon clear that these ancient scrolls included some of the oldest known texts of the Hebrew Bible ever found.

**983. More than two hundred biblical documents** have been found, some almost complete, written in both Hebrew and Aramaic—a Syrian language closely related to Hebrew, and the language spoken by Jesus. The Dead Sea Scrolls contain at least a portion of every book of the Hebrew Bible, except the Book of Esther.

**984. Among the Dead Sea Scrolls** is a complete "book" of Isaiah, composed of seventeen separate pieces of leather stitched together to form a roll nearly twenty-five feet long. Sophisticated dating techniques have proved that some of these scrolls were written nearly three hundred years before Jesus was born. Others came from Jesus' own lifetime.

**985. Copper scrolls** were also discovered in the Dead Sea caves at Qumran, describing a treasure—twenty-six tons of gold and sixty-five tons of silver—hidden at sixty-four locations throughout Israel. Most scholars believe the treasure is a hoax or myth, although others hold that the treasure was indeed taken from the temple and hidden before the Roman legions arrived in A.D. 70. It is very rare to find a Hebrew text on thinly beaten sheets of copper such as these.

RELATIONSHIP BETWEEN THE SHEPHERD AND THE SHEEP

**986. Palestine has always been known for large flocks of sheep,** and Arabs of the Bible lands have been largely dependent on sheep for their living throughout the centuries. The large number of sheep in the land can be understood when we read that Job had fourteen thousand sheep (Job 42:12), and that King Solomon, at the temple's dedication, sacrificed one hundred and twenty thousand sheep and goats (1 Kings 8:63).

**987. Fat-tailed sheep were the most common variety.** The fat tail provides reserve strength for the sheep, much like the hump does on a camel. When the sheep is butchered, this fatty tail is quite valuable. People will buy the tail, or part of it, and use it for frying. The Pentateuch makes reference to the fat tail of the sheep in Exodus 29:22, "Take from this ram the fat, the fat tail . . ."

**988. The youngest boy in the family becomes the shepherd** of the sheep. As the older son grows up he begins to help the father with sowing, plowing, and harvesting the crops, so he passes the shepherd tasks down to the younger brother and on down until the youngest of all becomes the family shepherd. Such was the custom when Jesse raised his family of eight sons. David was the youngest.

**989. The shepherd's scrip is a leather bag.** When he leaves home to tend the sheep, his mother will fill it with bread, cheese, dried fruit, and perhaps some olives. It was into a bag like this that David placed the five smooth stones when he went to battle with the giant Goliath.

**990. The Law of Moses speaks of tithing** (giving ten percent) from the flock. "The entire tithe of the herd and flock—every tenth animal that passes under the shepherd's rod—will be holy to the LORD" (Lev. 27:32). To do this Jewish writers tell us that the shepherd called the animals to him and as they would pass under his rod at a narrow entrance he would mark every tenth one with his rod, which had been dipped into a dye.

**991. More than a weapon.** From the story of David, we are familiar with the sling, but in addition to using a sling against wild animals or robbers, the shepherd found it very handy for directing the sheep. A stone could be dropped close to a sheep that was lagging behind and startle the sheep into coming along with the rest of the flock.

**992. In selecting pasture for the flock,** it is an absolute necessity that plenty of water is provided too. Flocks are often stationed near a stream of running water, but the sheep can be afraid of water that is running too quickly or that is roiled up with mud. The shepherd looks for pools of water or provides some quiet place where the sheep can quench their thirst.

**993. More than one flock may be kept in the same fold.** Often flocks are even mixed while being watered at a well. No attempt is made to separate them. When it is time to separate the sheep, one shepherd after another will stand up and call out: "Tahhoo! Tahhoo!" or a similar call of his own choice. The sheep will lift their heads, and after a scramble each one will begin following his master.

**994. The Eastern shepherd has a personal relationship** with his sheep that gives the figure of the Lord as the Shepherd of his people deep meaning. Not only does the shepherd often know his sheep by name, he never drives them, but leads them instead. This does not mean that he is always in front of them. He may walk by their side or sometimes follow behind.

**995. The shepherd is so acutely aware of each of his sheep** that often he doesn't even need to count them. He is able to feel the absence of any one of his sheep. When a shepherd of Lebanon was asked how he could keep track of his sheep if he didn't count, he replied, "If you were to put a cloth over my eyes, and bring me any sheep and only let me put hands on its face, I could tell in a moment if it was mine or not."

**996. The shepherd plays with the sheep** to pass the hours. A shepherd does this by pretending to run away. The sheep will soon overtake him and completely surround him, jumping and twisting with delight. The sheep know their shepherd will not leave them or turn them away.

## WEIGHTS AND MEASURES

**997. To measure length in the Old Testament** one would have used several units. From smallest to largest, the scale was finger-palm-span-cubit. The cubit was considered the most basic form of measurement, something like what Americans consider the "foot" measurement. The cubit was the length of the forearm measured to the tip of the middle finger. Generally this length varied between seventeen and eighteen inches in length.

**998. The span** was the distance from the tip of the thumb to the tip of the little finger with the hand extended and the fingers held apart. It was roughly one half of the standard cubit. The palm was approximately one sixth of the common cubit and was initially measured as the breadth of the hand at the base of the fingers. The finger measurement was considered to be about one quarter of a palm and was considered the smallest subdivision of the cubit.

**999. Weights** in the Bible followed their own system of measure. The weights ascended from the smallest weight of a pim, beka, or gerah, to the larger shekel, mina, and talent (as Jesus mentioned in one of the parables). For the smaller weights, balances would have been used to measure properly.

**1000. A shekel** was .403 ounces. The pim, beka, and gerah were all smaller fractions of the shekel. In order for these weights to be effective, balances were used. As the cubit was the standard measure, so the shekel was the standard unit of weight. Shekel is descended from the word meaning "to weigh."

**1001. The talent** was by far the largest unit of weight used to measure. Each talent was worth three thousand shekels and weighed around seventy-five pounds. Minas were between fifty and sixty shekels, depending on whether the system was Israelite or Babylonian. Each mina weighed roughly 1.25 pounds.

# Bibliography

The NIV Study Bible. © 1985 by The Zondervan Corporation. The Holy Bible, New International Version copyright © 1973, 1978, 1984 by International Bible Society.

Davis, Kenneth C. *Don't Know Much about the Bible: Everything You Need to Know about the Good Book but Never Learned.* New York: Eagle Brook, 1998.

Farb, Peter. *The Land, Wildlife, and Peoples of the Bible.* New York: Harper and Row, 1967.

Gantt, Michael. *A NonChurchgoer's Guide to the Bible.* Intercourse, Pa.: Good Books, 1977.

Packer, J. I., Merrill C. Tenney, and William White Jr. *Nelson's Illustrated Encyclopedia of Bible Facts.* Nashville: Thomas Nelson, 1980.

Paterson, John and Katherine. *Consider the Lilies: Plants of the Bible.* New York: Thomas Y. Crowell, 1986.

Phillips, Bob. *In Pursuit of Bible Trivia*. Eugene, Ore.: Harvest House, 1985.

Roberts, Jenny. *Bible Facts*. New York: Barnes and Noble, 1990.

Wight, Fred H. *Manners and Customs of Bible Lands*. Chicago: Moody, 1953.

*Mysteries of the Bible: The Enduring Questions of the Scriptures*. Pleasantville, N.Y.: Reader's Digest Books, 1988.

*Who's Who in the Bible: An Illustrated Guide*. New York: DK Publishing, 1998.

# Index

1001 Surprising
Things You Should
Know about
Christianity

*Jerry MacGregor and Marie Prys*

**This trove of fascinating facts—often humorous, always informative—offers a lively look at Christian history.**

Did you know . . . the first children's church was operated and attended solely by children and was held in a miniature church building with tiny pews? Or that the second-century church read from a book that was supposedly authored by the apostle Peter but was later rejected as forgery?

These are two of the many fun and revealing facts in *1001 Surprising Things You Should Know about Christianity.*

This lively and accessible collection is comprised of brief descriptions of things that make up Christendom. You'll find little-known facts as well as engaging explanations of well-known aspects of Christianity. These often-humorous tidbits cover culture, people, sayings, creeds and debates, churches, art and music, crusades, revivals, and more.

*1001 Surprising Things You Should Know about Christianity* is for everyone who enjoys history, theology, and interesting facts about the faith. It's also an excellent resource to share with your family, read in classrooms or small groups, use in a speech, or simply peruse for the fun of it!